Women's New Cinema in Contemporary Turkey

We can become harder to manage.
— SARA AHMED

Women's New Cinema in Contemporary Turkey

As If We Were Free, As If a Beautiful Life Were Possible

Pınar Fontini

EDINBURGH
University Press

Edinburgh University Press is one of the leading university presses in the UK. We publish academic books and journals in our selected subject areas across the humanities and social sciences, combining cutting-edge scholarship with high editorial and production values to produce academic works of lasting importance. For more information visit our website: edinburghuniversitypress.com

Grateful acknowledgement is made to the sources listed in the List of Illustrations for permission to reproduce material previously published elsewhere. Every effort has been made to trace the copyright holders, but if any have been inadvertently overlooked, the publisher will be pleased to make the necessary arrangements at the first opportunity.

The subtitle of this book is quoted with kind permission from Prof Saidiya Hartman.

Edinburgh University Press Ltd
13 Infirmary Street
Edinburgh EH1 1LT

First published in hardback by Edinburgh University Press 2025

Typeset in 10/13 Chaparral Pro by
IDSUK (DataConnection) Ltd, and
printed and bound by CPI Group (UK) Ltd,
Croydon, CR0 4YY

A CIP record for this book is available from the British Library

ISBN 978 1 3995 3849 7 (hardback)
ISBN 978 1 3995 3850 3 (paperback)
ISBN 978 1 3995 3851 0 (webready PDF)
ISBN 978 1 3995 3852 7 (epub)

MIX
Paper | Supporting responsible forestry
FSC
www.fsc.org
FSC® C013604

This book is printed using paper from well-managed forests, recycling and other controlled sources

Contents

Figures

Acknowledgments

Yeşim Ustaoğlu
Pelin Esmer
Belmin Söylemez
Zeynep Dadak
Handan İpekçi
Mizgin Müjde Arslan
Katoş
Audre Lorde
Sara Ahmed
Piraye Vera
Alba Ruiz de Luna Meyerhans
Aslı Gönül
Agnès Varda
James Fontini
Saidiya Hartman
Burcu Ovacık
Lina Koleilat
Mevlana
Fatoş Onul
bell hooks
Giada Ciampi
Rebecca Hill
Patricia White
Daguerréotypes
Academics of Boğaziçi University
Janice Loreck
Angie Black
RMIT University
Wendy Haslem
Nicolette Freeman
Sean Cubitt
Susan Lowish
University of Melbourne
Zeynep Çetin Erus
Elena Gorfinkel
Chris Berry
Ben Gook
My students
Bilge Karasu
Gloria Anzaldúa
Burgazada
Wimble St Northcote
Esra Biryıldız
Kübra Kelebekoğlu
King's College London
Sue Clayton
Dionne Brand
Belinda Glynn
Ocean Vuong
Gülsün Karamustafa
Ian Rafael Ramirez
Christina Sharpe
Nalan Abbasoğlu
Sibel Öz
Gillian Leslie
Edinburgh University Press
Sezin Romi
Salt Gallery
Sertaç Toksöz
Utku Gürler
Yalın Özgencil
Postbıyık Postproduction
Mabel Matiz
Muhammed Esed
Kınalıada
Gabrielle Grigg
Zagor & Maya
Mehdi Ait Oukhzame
Adana Golden Boll FF
Corey Cribb
Cristóbal Escobar
"forwards beckon rebound"
Rokia Traoré

Multiple places, things, and people sustained me during the writing of this book. I wrote the majority of it in the Princes' Islands during the pandemic. Writing about Turkey while living in it was the most intense part of this journey. I would like to thank my cat and the cats of the islands, my deep friends, and my niece for their love and wisdom in helping me to avoid the wear and tear Turkey can cause any minute, any day. There are songs, musicians, stories, and films referenced throughout the chapters. I thank the Sufi poets, queer artists, Black philosophers, and the storytellers of my land for their conviviality. Their company provided me with a kinder understanding of life and a more joyful understanding of creativity. And last of all, I would like to thank my students and my colleagues in Istanbul, London, and Melbourne who motivate my teaching, thinking, and filmmaking. These are my survival techniques and you are my inspiration. This research was supported by RMIT University (Research Allocation) and the University of Melbourne (Melbourne Research Scholarship)

Introduction: Şehnaz, Elmas, Mina, and the Others Who Kill the Angel in Their Houses

My mother was killed by the Angel in our house. I know many other women who were killed in the same way. Either to kill the Angel or be killed by her . . . It is a matter of life and death for us, for the women of Turkey. I am writing this book to introduce you to some of us: Şehnaz, Elmas, Mina, and several others who dare to choose life. They are the fictional and real female characters of the new wave films produced by the new generation of female directors from Turkey. I invite you to listen to their stories in which they tell the secrets of their houses, families, and nations. Their abiding by not the Angel but themselves might be a strategy to stay alive, even a method of radical existence.

As caught, killed, and revealed by Virginia Woolf, the Angel is an "intensely sympathetic," "immensely charming," and "utterly selfish" phantom (Woolf 1942). She is a phantom of a woman living under the same roof as Woolf. She is the perfect housewife, a sacrificing mother. As well as being dutiful, she is pure and graceful. The day when Woolf started writing the very first time, writing the words of a review of a novel written by a famous man, the Angel slips behind her and starts to whisper:

> My dear, you are a young woman. You are writing about a book that has been written by a man. Be sympathetic; be tender; flatter; deceive; use all the arts and wiles of our sex. Never let anybody guess that you have a mind of your own. Above all, be pure. (Woolf 1942)

Hearing the words of the Angel, Woolf turns upon her, catches her by the throat, and does her best to kill her. Woolf knows if she has not killed the Angel, she will be killed by her. But it is more difficult to kill a phantom than a reality. The Angel keeps appearing and reappearing; that is why Woolf has to repeat the act of killing several times to be able to kill her for real. This little story ends with Woolf saying: "But it was a real experience; it was an experience that was bound to befall all women writers at that time. Killing the Angel in the House was part of the occupation of a woman writer" (Woolf 1942).

Is not it worth considering that the age in which Woolf was alive has long gone, but the Angel continues haunting women's houses? Almost every house in

Turkey, whether it is in a city in western Turkey or a village in the east, has been haunted by this phantom. Sometimes the Angel appears on TV, disguised as a conservative politician, reminding us of the duties of pure and graceful women. Or at a dinner table, she whispers when to talk and when to nod and smile in silence.[1] Almost every house has its own Angel attempting to kill the women every day, every hour. But what sustains this Angel and who welcomes her into our houses?

Since being elected to power in 2002, the Justice and Development Party (JDP)[2] has extended its authoritarian regime in Turkey, reaching beyond the political sphere to include all aspects of society.[3] The policies of the JDP government do not recognize women as equal beings, instead considering them solely in their roles as wives, mothers, and daughters (İlkkaracan 2017, 62). The communities opposing the government directly (mainly queer people, women, Armenians and Kurds) have become "subject to intense religious and conservative pressure and 'otherization'" (2017, 67). However, thinking only of misogyny and a single power structure as the source of sexism in Turkey would provide us with a partial and limited understanding. In this story, there is more to see.

Co-opting the differences between its citizens, the state has been producing systematized oppression since its foundation, an oppression felt on all levels of culture, including and beyond cinema. Studies on how the subject, established as a historical category, is produced state that while building the nation-state, official (Kemalist) ideology created a discourse of an "internal enemy" and the very existence of Turkish society is made possible through the production of these internal enemies and enmities (Kaptanoğlu quoted in Ersoy 2019, 250). According to this understanding, "social schisms such as left versus right, Alevi versus Sunni, secular versus anti-secular, Turkish versus Kurdish, Muslim versus non-Muslim, were provoked [by the state] to the point of becoming blood feuds" (2019, 250). Yet, to comprehend the "psychic topography" of Turkey, it would be better to go beyond the idea that the subject is constructed merely through being hailed by a "crystalized power structure" (U. T. Arslan 2021). This can enable us to reach a more complicated web of relations and understand how the patriarchal, racist, and sexist norms are intertwined and how this is connected to us, ourselves, and the sustenance of the Angel inside our houses.

In the power-subject relationship, neither power succeeds in determining its subject completely, nor can the subject establish itself as a subject outside the structure (J. Butler 1997). The subject here is neither an entity produced entirely by the state nor able to exist outside of it. Understanding the construction of Turkishness as such, Umut Tümay Arslan attempts to explore its intricacies with a concept, "ethos of Turkishness" (U. T. Arslan 2022a). To Arslan, the ethos of Turkishness is "a form of social power" that is

> relational and has multiple fields, operating together with sexual politics, class, East-West asymmetry and fantasies, in short, social fault lines and antagonisms. It is less of a finished, completed, closed contract and more of a matrix that demands our continued investment and participation. (2022a)

In this exploration, Arslan invites us to see how this matrix is sustained by the interconnected racist, heterosexual, capitalistic, and patriarchal norms and our ongoing investment and participation in it.

I find this ethos of coexistence as the source keeping the Angel alive in Turkey for decades. Unlike Woolf's version, our Angel is not only a "white" problem. She has close connections with racist, hetero-patriarchal, and capitalistic norms integrated into our culture. Therefore, it is not some "evil other," but an "evil immanent in our culture in all its banality" (U. T. Arslan 2015) that welcomes the Angel; it is our complicity with such a culture that sustains this patriarchal norm about ideal feminine subjectivity. In this sense, the Angel is an extension of us, it is within ourselves. This understanding provides us with a better way to explore our psychic topography:

> While in one position I do not deny the forms of violence that establish Turkishness, or, for example, recognize the Kurds' struggle for dignity and establish emotional closeness, in another position I may continue to speak as a subject hailed by Turkishness. I may be the subject of knowledge about colonialism, orientalism, nationalism or hetero-patriarchal culture, but in an encounter that requires me to take myself into account, the power relations that have established me disappear into thin air—I may continue to experience a tremendous visual impairment, a selective blindness, in seeing that I am part of this network. (U. T. Arslan 2021)

But there are ways to invest in new possibilities, or as Christina Sharpe says, to "imagine otherwise" (Sharpe 2016). Imagining otherwise necessitates "noticing that ethos and habitus that already exist in our perspective" (U. T. Arslan 2015). Or as Audre Lorde says, it is about recognizing "that piece of the oppressor which is planted deep within each of us" ([1984] 2007, 208). The films of the new generation of female filmmakers in Turkey can be evaluated as part of such realization, a feminist intervention. The potentiality of their films in building new ways of seeing ourselves and each other which is different from the white heterosexual masculine gaze is my main motivation while writing this book and exploring their cinema.

There are other reasons why I chose to explore this topic in this book. Firstly, despite the restrictions faced by women in contemporary Turkey, there has been an unprecedented increase in the number of female directors in the first two decades of the twenty-first century.[4] These women not only occupy their own space and claim an authority of their own but also create a distinct cinema with feminist concerns. Within this book, I aim to understand how they produce films in an atmosphere of limitation and restriction and what stories, voices, and views they (re)present within their films. Leaving the Angel behind, how do their films imagine new possibilities and motivate new ways of seeing? How do the psycho-political dynamics of Turkey affect their production? And what contributions does their new cinema make to women's film culture worldwide?

Questions concerning female directors in Turkey and their work remain largely unconsidered and unanswered because recent scholarship predominantly conceptualizes contemporary Turkey's cinema in relation to a patriarchal discourse of white, heterosexual, and male auteurs and only recognizes female directors in a tokenistic manner. The existing literature is mainly authored by male historians and critics who have a tendency to take little care regarding the accuracy of the stories, achievements, and contributions of female directors (Fontini 2017, 1–6). As "the more he is cited, the more he is cited" (Ahmed 2017a), at the time of writing this book the film literature has almost no academic studies that approach female directors from Turkey holistically or define their narratives, styles, and production methods. In this sense, this book fills a significant gap in the existing literature, addressing and theorizing women's cinema in Turkey.

Critical Approach and Methodology

As in many non-Western regions, women's participation in directing films in Turkey was comparatively slow to arrive. The first time a female director directed a film in Turkey was in 1951, despite films having been produced by the national industry since 1896.[5] Both the quality and quantity of films directed by women have increased since then. Moreover, as I argue in this project, for the first time in the history of cinema, Turkey is witnessing a generation of female directors who create their own cinema with distinctive feminist features. However, these history-making female directors remain outsiders to the cinema of Turkey within the existing literature.

In this section, I detail the position of contemporary female directors, highlighting their status as under-examined in the cinema of Turkey. There are several sources theorizing Turkey's contemporary cinema (see Suner 2006a, 2010; Luxembourgeus and Baris 2018; Akser and Bayrakdar 2014; Dönmez-Colin 2008; Ottone 2017; S. Arslan 2011).[6] These books are quite useful for understanding the dynamics of new wave films made by male directors; a few even offer new critical approaches that include discourses of class, genre, and race, which is a novel way to evaluate the cinema of Turkey. However, although these authors claim that contemporary films provide an alternative discourse to mainstream cinema, they continue the patriarchal tradition of historiography by identifying the particularities of films made only by male directors. This method leaves a number of gaps and mistakes within the Turkish cinematic archives.

The existing film literature of Turkey already offers a misleading history making women's labor invisible. For instance, until the 1920s, Muslim Turkish women were not permitted to act in movies due to conservative limitations; therefore, non-Muslim Greek, Armenian, and Russian actresses were cast (Atakav 2013, 38). When Muslim actresses were finally cast in a film, it was the male director who was given credit by the critics, calling him "the pioneer director casting Muslim Turkish actresses for the first time" (Özgüç 1993, 16), while the contribution of the actresses remained unrecognized. There are similar examples within the history of female directors. When women finally started directing films in the 1950s, film critics took little care regarding their contributions to Turkey's cinema, leaving an incomplete cinematic archive to the present (Fontini 2017, 1–6). That is why each new female director from Turkey that emerged became identified as "the first female director, although they were not the first one" (Öztürk 2004, 33).

"The past that is not past reappears" (Sharpe 2016, 9). For the past not to reappear, I dedicate this book to the stories of contemporary female directors and their female characters which might disappear irretrievably otherwise. "Historical authenticity," says Michel-Rolph Trouillot, "resides not in the fidelity to an alleged past but in an honesty vis-a-vis the present as it re-presents that past" (1995, 148). Feminist historiography, in this sense, is not only about filling the gaps and silences in the past so as to correct the allegedly true history but also preserving the present so that the violence of the past does not repeat itself now. Pointing out the present absences and silences and making visible the invisible, this research can be a project to leave an alternative past, a less violent archive for the future.

Unlike the books mentioned above, there are several articles (see Öztürk 2010; İnceoğlu 2015; Kırel 2009; Koçer 2016; Dönmez-Colin 2010; Tanrıöver 2016) dedicated to the works of contemporary female directors. Some of these works provide a brief understanding of female directors' positions in the industry. However, they do not recognize the emergence of women's cinema and the rise of feminist film culture, and therefore fail to establish a holistic understanding of women's cinema in Turkey. There are also documentary films made about contemporary female filmmakers from Turkey. *Onun Filmi/Her First* was made by Su Baloğlu and Merve Bozcu in 2019 and I made *Senin Yıllardır Gerçekleştirmeyi*

Beklediğin Bir Düş Var/Dream Workers in 2022. This highlights the gap identified in this research. Contemporary female filmmakers from Turkey and their films are under-examined in national and international film literature and under-represented in Turkish audiovisual history.

Examining contemporary women's cinema enables correcting an injustice that ignores the work of women directors. It also allows us to enter into a new world in which we can explore new perspectives on film methodology, narrative, characterization, documentary style, and filmmaking practice as well as collaboration, feminism, resistance, and Turkey's identity. These are some of the highlights this book explores while identifying the particularities of the emerging women's cinema in Turkey. For these analyses, I adapt a critical feminist lens and use concepts and arguments of a feminist film theory that has strong connections with the white Western academy. However, most of the feminist debates in this book do not travel to Turkey from the West. Learning feminism from her aunt who is a brown Muslim woman from Pakistan, Sara Ahmed says:

> It might be assumed that feminism travels from West to East. It might be assumed that feminism is what the West gives to the East. That assumption is a traveling assumption, one that tells a feminist story in a certain way, a story that is much repeated; a history of how feminism acquired utility as an imperial gift. That is not my story. We need to tell other feminist stories. (Ahmed 2017b, 4)

Like Ahmed, this book finds feminism not in stories traveled from the West but in stories told by contemporary women filmmakers from Turkey. It chooses to introduce these feminist narratives by adopting concepts created by authors from Turkey such as Umut Tümay Arslan (2021; 2022a; 2022b; 2022c), Feride Çiçekoğlu (2015), and Nurdan Gürbilek (2001; 2012; 2015). Translating their texts provides me not only with the vocabulary to tell an "other" feminist story but also with an understanding of the cultural and political sicknesses and weaknesses of Turkish society that affect the relationship between women and cinema. Introducing these films with the terminology of these authors, this project enables "other feminist stories" to travel toward the rest of the world.

As many (feminist) film theories born in the white Western academies do not work fully to explore the filmmaking practices of contemporary female directors from Turkey, I also work closely with Black feminist genealogy and adopt concepts and theories developed by Audre Lorde, Sara Ahmed, bell hooks, Toni Morrison, Christina Sharpe, and Saidiya Hartman. These authors, together with postcolonial and post-third worldist feminist scholars such as Gloria Anzaldúa, Marnia Lazreg, Chandra Mohanty, Cherríe Moraga, Trinh T. Minh-ha, and Ella Shohat, bring multicultural, postcolonial, and intersectional theories into feminist and film discussions by examining the terms "power," "relationality," and "intersectionality." They also enable me to create new critical concepts such as "accented feminism" and "accented feminist film criticism" which will be explored in more detail in Chapter 3. These new critiques not only add a gender dimension into the diasporic film theory but also extend feminist film theory by adding the racial dimension into the discussion. This is my intervention in the whiteness of feminist film theory which dismisses the racial and "national" conditions. The new critical frameworks introduced in this book also enable a more precise discussion of the conditions of production for non-Western films while providing the tools to conduct textual and stylistic analysis of them.

Working on women's film culture in Turkey while currently located in Australia enables me to analyze Turkey's actualities more precisely. Experiencing "breathlessness" (see Sharpe 2016) while living under an authoritarian regime in Turkey, we fail to live life and understand it simultaneously. In this project, I will attempt to do what we are used to failing at "home": analyze our experiences critically and generate theoretical knowledge from our lives. For this, I will work through "lived theory" (Frye 1991, 13), which understands that "theory can do more the closer it gets to the skin" (Ahmed 2017b, 10). The intellectual tradition expects theory to be abstract, it assumes that "something is more theoretical the more abstract it is, the more it is abstracted from everyday life" (2017b, 10). Rather than dragging theory away from life, I prefer following Black feminist and feminist of color scholarship and consider "the personal" as "theoretical" (2017b, 10). I take theory as a "necessary practice" and understand personal experience as a "fertile ground for the production of liberatory feminist theory" (hooks 1991, 1). Those who encounter the violence of the state in various ways—women, queers, Kurds, and others—and are hurt so intensely can find liberation in theory. We can see in theory "a location for healing" (1991, 1).

The theory, in return, provides us with knowledge of ourselves. And by understanding our inmost selves, we understand our surroundings; that is why I write as a queer, feminist, working class, and white-skinned (not white; see Morales 1981, 91) scholar and filmmaker who is from the "inside." By "writing as," I do not give up my objective position; rather, I make myself engaged and accountable. Donna Haraway says:

> Location is about vulnerability; location resists the politics of closure, finality, or to borrow from Althusser, feminist objectivity resists "simplification in the last instance." That is because feminist embodiment resists fixation and is insatiably curious about the webs of differential positioning. There is no single feminist standpoint because our maps require too many dimensions for that metaphor to ground our visions. But the feminist standpoint theorists' goal of an epistemology and politics of engaged, accountable positioning remains

> eminently potent. The goal is better accounts of the world, that is, "science." (Haraway 1988, 590)

Feminist objectivity is not a Western mode of impartiality. As Gloria Anzaldúa says, "In trying to become 'objective, Western culture made 'objects' of things and people when it distanced itself from them, thereby losing 'touch' with them. This dichotomy is the root of all violence" (1987, 37). Rather than searching in distance and losing touch with things and people, I research in proximity and relation by including my personal. "Autobiographical example is not a personal story that folds onto itself; it's not about navel gazing," says Saidiya Hartman and continues, "it's really about trying to look at historical and social process and one's own formation as a window onto social and historical processes, as an example of them" (Hartman quoted in Saunders 2008, 7). Locating my feminist story with all its heterogeneity as one of the positions amongst many, I aim "to tell a story capable of engaging and countering the violence of abstraction" (Hartman quoted in Saunders 2008, 7).

I would like to end this section by adding the questions "to whom" to speak and "why", next to the question of "how to speak." It might feel dangerous what I do, thinking in Turkish and writing in English, as "we fear those who speak about us who do not speak to us and with us" (hooks 1990, 343). Sara Ahmed eases my concern with her notion of a "feminist ear." Ahmed thinks that "a feminist ear can be how you hear what is not being heard," or having a feminist ear is to begin to hear how women are not heard (Ahmed 2017b, 202–3). This book provides an opportunity for feminist ears to listen to the stories of women from Turkey. I would like to invite the feminist ears into this book in which we can collectively listen to what has not been heard before: the dreams, experiences, imaginations, and insights of contemporary female filmmakers from Turkey. Realizing the "impossible" and the "necessary" (see Hartman quoted in Bulley 2020) by attempting a feminist film culture under an authoritarian regime, these filmmakers might help us to "imagine otherwise" (Sharpe 2016). I would like to welcome you to this space where we can meditate on the capacity of the "as if" depicted in their films: "as if we were free, as if a beautiful life were possible" (Hartman quoted in Bulley 2020).

Women's New Cinema: "As If We Were Free, As If a Beautiful Life Were Possible"

This book identifies the new production methods and stylistic approaches used by contemporary female directors from Turkey in relation to sociopolitical and cultural dynamics and conceptualizes these features under the term "Women's

New Cinema." Drawing a frame for the concept "Women's New Cinema," I identify the commonalities amongst the filmmaking practices and filmographies of contemporary female directors from Turkey. In venturing this new term and including new perspectives in it, my aim is to stage a critical intervention into the evaluation of contemporary female directors and their films within the Turkish context. To be able to explore the particularities of the new term "Women's New Cinema," I should like to start with the following questions: what is women's cinema,[7] what is new here, and what is the category "women"?

> In a world overflowing with images and representations, who do we fail to see or comprehend? What could be the consequences of this selective blindness? How are visibility and audibility possible? For whom? By whom? Or whose visibility and audibility can we talk about? Who is invisible to whom? How do we bear witness to the world? How do we see, how are we seen? Since we live with visual technologies and visualization practices: How to see? Why is it seen? What are the limits of vision? What is it seen for? Who is seen with? Who gets more than one perspective? Who gets blindfolded? Who wears blinders? Who interprets the visual field? Besides vision, which sensory abilities would we like to develop? Or: How can we combat violent, conquering mirrors of self? (Haraway quoted in U. T. Arslan 2022c)

These questions provide answers to my questions. Understanding women's cinema as a question/becoming/under construction rather than fixed/monolithic/complete, I will come back to these questions again and again throughout this book. As well as being asked (by Haraway) to "establish a science of life that better explains the world," they are also the questions of "feminist praxis," "women's cinema," and "feminist narrative" which seek another kind of "seeing," "hearing," and "record-keeping" (U. T. Arslan 2022c). These questions are not just rhetorical, which is why they can provide us with ideas that are dynamic rather than fixed. Like women's cinema, they provoke us to think without providing us with a conclusive statement.

The questions, together with potential answers and potential new questions, enable me to complicate the category of women in women's cinema and include the notions of race, class, and sexuality in feminist film studies, which is a methodology we owe to Black feminist epistemology. Understanding the intersections of race, class, gender, and sexuality as a possibility to "come into contact with those who are stopped by what allowed us to pass through," I aim to reveal the forces that allow "others" to pass but stop females from Turkey without ignoring the fact that these "others" "have the experience of being stopped," too (Ahmed 2016, 23). This approach is about recognizing that we are different from each other, but we are similar in being the other. As AnaLouise Keating says "while our lives and our experiences might be widely divergent, we are all, in various ways, the product of a racist/sexist/oppressive social system" (2013, 41). Or, "we're all in the same boat," as Rosario Morales suggests in *This Bridge Called My Back* (Morales 1981, 91). Shifting its politics from "binary-oppositional" to "radical interconnectivity" (Keating 2013, 52), which is a relational approach recognizing the commonalities between us without ignoring our differences, this book wants to embrace what unravels when we happen upon each other. Within this "affinity" (see Ahmed 2016), the experiences of female directors from Turkey may build more bridges between us and offer a site for transnational and feminist exchange.

This approach also allows me to think through experiences based on contextual realities and gives me the vocabulary to talk about the present and the actual which is a must and urgent. Only by adopting an intersectional approach does the theoretical concept of "Women's New Cinema" gain the capacity to talk about the captured, projected, and witnessed life experiences of Kurdish women, Muslim women, Kurdish transexual women, Alevi women, peasant women, Armenian women and Greek women, working-class women, and white Turkish women. That is why "Women's New Cinema," first and foremost, points to a cinematic space occupied by women that is fundamentally different from the cinematic realm created by the previous generation of female directors from Turkey.[8] The films of the female directors of previous decades commonly used stereotypical images of an ideologically laden femininity, featuring women in traditional, limited roles. In contrast, contemporary female filmmakers from Turkey conceptualize female images as constructed socially and historically, featuring female protagonists with agency and producing films addressing female audiences. The distinct storytelling, including the narrative and style, together with the diversity of female subjectivities, including those of the directors, point to a "new" cinematic era for female directorship which has the potential to challenge the male-dominated and homogenous (racially, sexually, and religiously) ideological structure of Turkey. However, women's cinema in Turkey is not simply a reaction to current power structures. It imagines new horizons of the possible by adopting politics of hope. The hope here, as Bronwyn Carlson and Ryan Frazer state, is not "a form of naïve or politically impotent optimism" but about keeping the future open to difference (2021, 241). In this sense, Women's New Cinema is a radical expression of another possibility.

Contemporary women's cinema in Turkey also shares similarities with the new wave films of the New Cinema Movement. In the mid-1990s, a new mode of filmmaking called the New Cinema Movement emerged in Turkey. The films belonging to this mode of production have personalized narratives and an independent, minimalistic style (Suner 2006a, 33). It is a self-reflective cinema issuing themes related to cultural, social, and national identity and belonging (Ottone 2017, 9–12). Unlike the mainstream films produced and distributed by major companies such as United International Pictures (UIP) and Warner Brothers (WB), these independent art films were funded by newly emerging funding and festival networks such as the Cultural Ministry, Eurimages, and international film festivals. The production dynamics, independent filmmaking methods, and minimalist features used by contemporary female filmmakers in Turkey align with the modes of production of the New Cinema Movement. However, their storytelling, with feminist discourse and the feminist concerns of their aesthetics, contribute to women's film culture. This separates their cinema from patriarchal modes and codes of storytelling. Enabling us to imagine new things or imagine things in a new way also makes their cinema "new," leading to the term "Women's New Cinema." The term is used to describe the work of contemporary female filmmakers in Turkey and signify the birth of a women's cinema which is also "new" for the Turkish context.

Industrial Framework

Turkey has never had an autonomous cinema industry; it has always been affected by political and economic interventions.[9] The contemporary cinematic landscape has been shaped by similar dynamics. Starting from the 1990s until today, the major distributors and the products of Hollywood have dominated the local Turkish market. This not only affects the distribution and exhibition conditions of domestic films but it also "Americanizes" the visual taste of the audience and changes patterns of behavior towards a more consumerist culture (Fontini 2017, 62). Filled with local and American blockbusters, the domestic market does not accommodate Turkish independent films.

As independent producers cannot earn enough money from box office revenues to invest in new films, new financial modalities have emerged. The funding support provided by TV channels, the Cultural Ministry, sponsors, and Eurimages brought out a new mode of production. Unlike the Yeşilçam model (the commercial Turkish cinema), in which it was the distributors and exhibitors raising the production budget from ticket sales, it was the director-producers raising the funding through applying different sources. This director-producer model allowed many women filmmakers to enter the industry. From 1950 to 1990, the total number of women directors was ten. The years 1990 to 2000, however, Turkey witnessed fourteen women filmmakers who started their careers. Six of them, Tomris Giritlioğlu, Biket İlhan, Seçkin Yasar, Handan İpekçi, Yeşim Ustaoğlu, and Necef Uğurlu, established production companies to produce the films they directed; these companies are, respectively, Sis Yapım, Sinevizyon, Amenis, Yeni Yapım Film, Ustaoğlu Film Production, and Grup Üç

Ajans. Two of them, Canan Gerede and Fide Motan, produced/co-produced their films without establishing companies, while the remaining few worked with a producer (Fontini 2017, 179–454). The increase in the number of female filmmakers makes it clear that in the previous industry model, women filmmakers were not preferred by producers, who were dominantly male; only ten women filmmakers had emerged in forty years, while fourteen emerged in the 1990s with the introduction of a new production model.

The diversity of funding also brought out a new filmmaking model conceptualized under the term, New Cinema Movement. The most prominent feature of this movement was the evolution of cinema; from actors' cinema to directors' cinema (Erkılıç 2003, 154). On one hand, auteur directors started making independent, art house films. As they became free from the box office revenue, they were not dependent on the preferences of the audience (Pösteki 2005, 50), which meant that they did not have to be commercially successful. This led to different modes of marketing and distribution strategies (Zaim 2008, 48) and freedom in content and style. Realizing their films with low budgets, these independent filmmakers adopted a minimalist style and cast amateur actors; they problematized social issues, the effects of the eighties coup, workers conditions and identity (with new characters: Kurds, Armenians, homosexuals) in character-based narratives (Orta 2012, 174–5). As they did not have the chance to be screened in movie theatres, they created their own medium: festivals. Screened at national and international film festivals such as Antalya Golden Orange Film Festival, Berlinale, and Cannes, they raised the reputation of the national cinema and brought international recognition.

This book analyzes the aesthetics and production models of six contemporary women filmmakers who not only contribute to the New Cinema Movement but also are giving rise to a feminist film culture in Turkey. The following chapters explore aspects of their work from the content and style of their films to representation and the conditions of production. The directors whose work has been selected for analysis are Pelin Esmer, Yeşim Ustaoğlu, Handan İpekçi, Zeynep Dadak, Mizgin Müjde Arslan, and Belmin Söylemez. While some of these filmmakers are established, some are mid and early career filmmakers. The book pays attention to both fiction and non-fiction films they produce. By choosing a diverse range of films and filmmakers, this study aims to bring a holistic understanding to contemporary women's film culture in Turkey.

Chapter Breakdown

This book argues that contemporary women filmmakers, for the first time in history, are creating a feminist film culture in Turkey. Analyzing the themes, styles, and production patterns of contemporary women's cinema in Turkey, I have identified six categories defining emerging women's cinema as a distinct category. These six distinctive characteristics (space, directorial persona, female representation, political aesthetics, diversity, and industry) are explored in detail in each chapter of this book through case studies. Feminist textual analysis is used to explore the film texts and examine the production methods of six contemporary female directors whose films highlight the six characteristics under examination. The directors who participated in this research were also interviewed and extracts from these interviews are used throughout the book. In the chapters, I mention other contemporary women's films from Turkey as examples to support my explorations. As this research is entangled with my own subjective experience of being a queer, female filmmaker and scholar from Turkey, I also use my own journey as a source to construct knowledge.

The first chapter of this book, "Burning Down the House: The Snapping Female Figure and Her Haphazard Wanderings," argues that Women's New Cinema offers its audience a new story by building an alternative relationship between women and space. For this, it examines *Şimdiki Zaman/Present Tense* made by Belmin Söylemez in 2012. Unlike the traditional and patriarchal narratives, Söylemez uses an alternative understanding of space to offer her audience a different story; in this story, the danger stems from the familiar—home, family, and country—the "new Turkey." The chapter argues that home, family, and nation/country looking familial and friendly are indeed unsettling in contemporary women's cinema. That is why the female figure of Women's New Cinema breaks from these damaging ties and domestic tasks; she leaves the Angel behind and wanders haphazardly in the streets, the "space of happenstance." The uncanny corners of the space or the "terrible beauty" (see Moten 2017; Hartman 2020) enable her to become someone new. At the end of the story, it is not her husband or her children but herself that transforms. Capturing the essence of the current atmosphere of Turkey, this new relationship reflects the diversity of lived experiences of women (either in the city or in town), making the audience confront the ongoing hardship of living within the confines of a patriarchal society.

Belmin Söylemez is the director of *Present Tense*. She is known for her short films, documentaries, and fiction films. Her short films and documentaries have been screened in international film festivals such as Toronto, Gothenburg, and Sarajevo, and received a number of awards nationally and internationally. Her work has been broadcast on TV channels such as ARTE France/Germany, SVT (Sweden), YLE (Finland), SBS (Australia). Her films have also participated in exhibitions such as "Call me Istanbul," ZKM Karlsruhe, Germany, and "Free Kick"—the 9th Istanbul Biennial. Her first feature-length fiction film *Present*

Tense won the prestigious New Director's Prize at the 56th San Francisco International Film Festival and was also crowned with the Yılmaz Güney Special Jury Award and Critics Prize in the National Competition of the 22nd Golden Boll Film Festival. The film also brought Sanem Öge best actress awards at the 31st Istanbul Film Festival and the 24th Ankara Film Festival. Söylemez released her second film, *Mirror Mirror*, in 2022 and won Avni Tolunay Jury Special Award at the 59th International Antalya Golden Orange Film Festival.

Chapter 2, "Companions of Nesibe: Female Representation in Women's New Cinema," focuses on female representation by applying a critical analysis of Yeşim Ustaoğlu's film *Tereddüt/Clair Obscur* (2016). Chapter 2 argues that Women's New Cinema challenges the traditional portrayal of women in male-dominated films, which often depict them as passive, faithful, and obedient. Instead, the chapter contends that Women's New Cinema reconstructs a new female image characterized by her agency. The chapter investigates this new depiction, which represents a more nuanced characterization than women in older Turkish films, using the notions of Teresa De Lauretis (1984; 1990a), Anneke Smelik (1998), and Asuman Suner (2006a). Contemporary female Turkish directors create this new image by telling women-centered stories. The female directors portray a female image not as an object or a fetish but as a character whose experiences assign meaning to the film. These new films construct the feminist subject as the producer of meaning, the narratives are designed to narrate the story from the female point of view. The directors present stories strengthened by female solidarity instead of creating conflicts between good and bad women or urban and traditional women. Contemporary female directors portray the female image as a "historical and social subject," mirroring the ongoing struggles of the feminist agenda in Turkey. Each female character's individual challenges offer a microcosm of "being a woman" in Turkey. By depicting diverse female identities, including working class, Greek or Kurdish, non-Muslim, or women with different sexual orientations or identities, Women's New Cinema breaks free from one-dimensional representation and reflects a more complex characterization than women from earlier Turkish films.

Yeşim Ustaoğlu is an established filmmaker who has made films since the 1990s. She received international recognition for her 1999 film *Journey to The Sun*, which competed at the Berlinale and received the Blue Angel Award (Best European Film) and the Peace Prize before sweeping the Istanbul Film Festival, winning Best Film, Best Director, the FIPRESCI Prize and the Audience Award. Her third film, *Waiting for the Clouds*, was shown at the 2005 Berlinale Panorama and was awarded the annual Sundance/NHK International Filmmaker's Award. Ustaoglu's fourth feature, *Pandora's Box*, premiered in Toronto (Toronto International Film Festival) and won the Golden Shell for the Best Film and Silver

Shell for the Best Actress awards at the San Sebastian Film Festival. Her fifth feature, *Somewhere in Between*, premiered in the Orrizonti section at the 69th Venice Film Festival, won the Best Film Award at the Abu Dhabi Film Festival and the Split Mediterranean Film Festival, as well as Best Performance at the Moscow, Tokyo, and Pune film festivals. Her latest film is *Clair Obscur.*

Chapter 3, "Her Resistance is Many: The Accented Filmmaking Practice in Women's New Cinema," discusses that unlike the majority of narratives centering on the stories of white Turks, Women's New Cinema invites the audience to listen to the stories of vulnerable communities. "Her Resistance is Many" analyses the documentary, *Ez Firiyam Tu Mayî Li Cî/I Flew You Stayed* (2012) made by the Kurdish filmmaker Mizgin Müjde Arslan. In this documentary, Arslan deploys a double-sided critique, that is, criticizing the feudal structure of her own nationality/ethnicity while simultaneously criticizing Turkish nationalism and hegemonic Eurocentric and Turkish feminism. To explore this double-edged critique, I apply the principles of accented film theory developed by Hamid Naficy. However, Naficy's critical framework lacks attention to gender. Adding the perspectives of academics of color and postcolonial feminist scholars such as Inderpal Grewal and Caren Kaplan, Chandra Mohanty, Ella Shohat and Sara Ahmed, I develop a new concept: "accented feminist film criticism." The concept includes the dimension of gender in the accented and diasporic film discussions by articulating the significance of differences based on race, ethnicity, class, and sexuality in gender discourse. Only this new framework enables the examination of the accented female filmmakers from Turkey. Voicing the stories of the vulnerable other, the "accented imaginary" created by the accented female filmmakers not only transforms what cinema is in contemporary Turkey but is also transformative of society, and history.

Mizgin Müjde Arslan is a mid-career director whose latest film is *I Flew You Stayed.* She was born in Mardin, a city located in the Kurdish region of Turkey. She received various national and international awards with her first short film, *The Last Game*. Her first documentary, *A Fatal Dress, Polygamy*, premiered at the Istanbul Film Festival and was broadcast on TV 24 and IMC TV. Her first feature documentary, *I Flew, You Stayed*, has won a number of awards, including the Turkish Association of Film Critics, Documentary of the Year (2013), and Mirella Galetti Award in Italy in 2014. The short film *Houses with Small Windows*, which she co-wrote and acted in, was selected for Official Competition at the Venice Film Festival (2013) and won the European Short Film Award as well as many other awards. Arslan received the Sundance Institute Documentary Fund in 2023 to realize her next project, *My Mothers' Tale*.

Chapter 4, "'The Master's Tools Will Never Dismantle the Master's House': The Political Aesthetics of Women's New Cinema," offers a discussion on the political aesthetics (anti-oppressive, feminist, and ethical filmmaking models) of Women's New Cinema by focusing on *Mavi Dalga/The Blue Wave* made by Zeynep Dadak and Merve Kayan (2013). For this, the chapter uses the concept "open image," which is developed by Shohini Chaudhuri and Howard Finn. Applying the concept of "open image," the chapter analyses the usage of the dull, banal happenings of the everyday, telling the story of the "ordinary," the dedramatized narrative structure, the unaesthetization of the female body, unsympathetic characters, failure of identification, using a cyclic time and cyclic rhythm which are the aesthetic tactics adapted by contemporary female filmmakers from Turkey. The chapter explores whether these directors use these aesthetic strategies to destabilize hegemonic, sexist language, allowing the audience to see the world in a new way. The filmmakers make anti-oppressive, feminist, and ethical filmmaking models visible on the national cinematic scene. In this chapter, by adding political and feminist values to it, the chapter also changes and enlarges the concept of "open image" although Chaudhuri and Finn use the term as an apolitical aesthetic form.

Zeynep Dadak is a new generation filmmaker and the co-director of *The Blue Wave*. After studying Cinema at Marmara University, she continued her doctoral studies at New York University, in the Cinema Studies department. Besides writing reviews in *Altyazı* cinema magazine and lecturing on film at various universities, she continues making documentaries and short films. *Çalıştır Saksıyı* (2001), *Gidiş Geliş Gidiş* (2004), and *Tarihe Şerh: Irak Dünya Mahkemesi* (2007) are her short films; in 2010, she made a documentary film with Kayan, *Bu Sahilde/On the Coast*. In 2020, she made the documentary *Ah Gözel İstanbul/Invisible to the Eye*. Merve Kayan was born in 1981 in Edirne, Uzunköprü. She received her FA in Visual Arts at University of California, San Diego. Her short films are *Aud* (2003), *The Gift* (2003), *Sweet Splits* (2005, co-director), *Ah* (2006), and *Work* (2008).

Chapter 5, "'Because Of Her, We Can': Subjectivity and Collectivity in Women's New Cinema," focuses on the subjectivity of the director and the emancipation of the female spectator in Women's New Cinema in the documentary film *Oyun/The Play* (2005) made by Pelin Esmer. To analyze the subjectivity of the director, the chapter creates a new framework: "experiential mode." Within this mode, it formulates the subjectivity of the filmmaker through understanding filmmaking as a practice to be experienced and interacted with rather than a way of looking and showing. By adapting the concepts of authors such as Audre Lorde ([1984] 2007), Katherine McKittrick (2021), Christina Sharpe (2023), and AnaLouise Keating (2013), the chapter discusses "erotic," "wonder," "coincidentiality," "care," and "raw intention" as the sources of experiential mode of filmmaking. It also discusses the subjectivity of the female audience. Thinking through the ideas of Jacques Rancière (2009), the chapter explores the viewing experience as something active instead of evaluating it as being in a passive state. Communicating with the audience through the female character, the female filmmaker creates a space where the meaning is "negotiated." The chapter concludes that this perspective dismantles the rigid binaries such as the producer and consumer, active and passive, and opens the doors of a non-hierarchical space that can be the place of feminist ethics.

Pelin Esmer is an established director who produces her films with her production company Sinefilm. Since 2001, she has made *The Collector*, *The Play*, *10 to 11*, *Watchtower*, *Something Useful*, and *Queen Lear*. The feature documentary *The Play* made its international premiere at the San Sebastian Film Festival. It has been screened at over fifty festivals around the world and received many awards including Best New Documentary Filmmaker Award at the Tribeca Film Festival. Her first fiction, *10 to 11*, was one of the six projects chosen by the Cannes Film Festival's Résidence du Cinéfondation in Paris where she worked on the script. Her second fiction, *Watchtower*, which was premiered in Toronto and at the Rotterdam Film Festival, has been screened in many countries and five different US states as part of the Caravanserai Program. *Something Useful* received the Best Screenplay award at the Tallinn International Film Festival as well as FIPRESCI, Best Director, Best Screenplay, and Best Actress awards in Turkey. In 2018, Pelin Esmer was invited to Berlin by the DAAD Artists-in-Residence Program where she developed her last documentary film, *Queen Lear*.

Chapter 6, "Her Existence is Resistance: Being a Female Director in the Turkish Film Industry," explores the effect of industrial dynamics over the story of Handan İpekçi. It examines how a "difficult" positionality (both nationally and internationally) complicates the independent production processes of contemporary female filmmakers from Turkey. "Her Existence is Resistance" concludes that Women's New Cinema needs more support from European funding bodies to stay alive by investigating the problematic parts of the Turkish film industry such as its financial dependency on the Cultural Ministry. However, the international funding mechanisms are also problematic due to the expectations of funding bodies. As in the West, Middle Eastern and Muslim women are denied an identity in the plural and women artists from the same region are expected to reproduce stereotypical Middle Eastern femininity. This last chapter highlights the importance of discussing these problems for non-Western female filmmakers to be able to stay independent.

Handan İpekçi made her debut as a film director in 1993 with the documentary *Song of the Kemenche*. A year later in 1994, she shot her first feature *Dad is in the Army*, a reflection on the 1980 military coup through the eyes of children. Her controversial feature *Big Man Little Love, Hejar* (2001), which she wrote, produced, and directed, was Turkey's official submission for the 74th Academy Awards in the Best Foreign Language Film category, and went on to win Best Film and Best Script awards in Antalya. She released *Çınar Ağacı/The Plane Tree* in 2011.

The book closes with an Epilogue presenting selections from interviews with these filmmakers in a roundtable discussion mode. The interviews reveal their filmmaking processes in their own voices. Using narratives to construct knowledge and placing "personal" stories at the core of this research, this book interrogates the idea that when it is *his* story, it easily becomes History but when it is *our* story—that is, queers, women, Blacks, Muslims, and so on—it always remains a personal story. This book contributes to History through our "personal" stories.

Notes

1. Feminist killjoy is a subversive figure to this stereotyping patriarchal system. Inspired by Ama Ata Aidoo who repurposed the figure of killjoy in her novel *Our Sister Killjoy* (Aidoo [1977] 1994), Sara Ahmed introduces the figure of the feminist killjoy in her book *The Promise of Happiness* (2010) and makes her legible in her latest book, *The Feminist Killjoy Handbook* (2023). The feminist figure kills the joy simply by *not* joining the invitations of the patriarchal system. In other words, the feminist killjoy kills the Angel so as not to be killed by her.
2. The Turkish name of the Justice and Development Party (JDP) is Adalet ve Kalkınma Partisi.
3. When it came to power in 2002, the JDP declared its political ideology as a "conservative democracy." This ideology is "unlike the European notion of conservatism, which aims at upholding traditional economic and political institutions. It is much more similar to American social conservatism with a primary focus on conservative social policies specifically regarding gender equality, the status of women and LGBTI+ people" (İlkkaracan 2017, 63). After its second term (2007–11), the party's self-proclaimed "conservative democracy" (Özbudun 2006; Duran 2008) took an "authoritarian turn" (Benhabib 2013).
4. It was not until the 1950s that the first female director made a film in Turkey. From the 1950s until the 1990s, the number of female directors was consistently low. There were only two female directors in the 1950s (Cahide Sonku and Nuran Şener); three new female directors in the 1960s (Feyturiye Esen, Bilge Olgaç, and Birsen Kaya); three new female directors in the 1970s (Lale Oraloğlu, Türkan Şoray, and Ayten Ürkmez-Kuyululu); and two new female directors in the 1980s (Nisan Akman and Mahinur Ergun). In the 1990s, Turkey witnessed fourteen debut female directors (Füruzan, Gülsün Karamustafa, Canan Gerede, Tomris Giritlioğlu, Işıl Özgentürk, Biket İlhan, Seçkin Yasar, Handan İpekçi, Canan Evcimen, Fide Motan, Yeşim Ustaoğlu, Sunar Kural Aytuna, Necef Uğurlu, and Jülide Övür). Since the 2000s, an unprecedented number of female directors have emerged.

5. Understanding the reasons for such delays necessitates considering the sociopolitical context as well as the dynamics of the male-dominated film industry. Please see *Celluloid Ceiling: Women Film Directors Breaking Through* (Kelly and Robson 2014) for an extensive evaluation of non-Western female directors and pioneers.
6. *Kadının Kamerasından: 2000 Sonrası Kadın Yönetmenler* (Sönmez and Satıcı 2019) is a recent book examining particularities of the films made by female directors based on feminist film theory. However, the contents of the chapters are independent of each other, and the book fails to conceptualise the distinct features of women's cinema in Turkey.
7. The question of women's cinema has been a central debate since the beginning of 1970s. Major contributors to the arguments are Claire Johnston ([1973] 1999), Laura Mulvey ([1975] 1999), Teresa De Lauretis (1984; [1985] 2007), Anneke Smelik (1998), Lucy Fisher (1989), Judith Mayne (1990), Sandy Flitterman-Lewis (1990), Annette Kuhn (1994), Patricia Mellencamp (1995), Tania Modleski (1999), Alison Butler (2002), and Patricia White (2015).
8. From 1951 until 2000, there were only twenty-four women filmmakers. Of these, only a few directors—Bilge Olgaç, Mahinur Ergun, Nisan Akman, Gülsün Karamustafa and Füruzan, and Işıl Özgentürk—displayed complex female subjectivities in their films (Fontini 2017; Öztürk 2004).
9. Sources about the Turkish film industry in English are limited. For more detail on this topic, see the report prepared by Martin Kanzler (2014), which includes not only information on the dynamics of production, distribution, and exhibition but also a historic overview of the industry.

Chapter 1

Burning Down The House: The Snapping Female Figure and Her Haphazard Wanderings

After completing my master's thesis, I decided to continue my academic journey in the same department at the same university in Istanbul as a PhD candidate. It was the summer of 2017; the morning was rising on my favorite walking trail in Istanbul when I received a message from the institution. It notified me that my candidature had become invalid. It was invalidated because of a speech made by the head of the cinema department who was the committee member validating my candidature. Her speech supported the academics who had been fired from their departments for signing a petition suggesting a peaceful solution to the Kurdish–Turkish conflict. I was fired from my candidature because of a speech made by an academic supporting the academics having been fired because of signing a peace petition. During that walk, I decided to leave Turkey in order to not to leave the work I wanted to do. Two years later, I and my favorite authors packed in my luggage flew almost 15,000 kilometers away from Istanbul. The next day, I found myself in Melbourne, Australia, and went to meet my PhD supervisor.

Such a story! This is clearly the story of an academic from a country called "new Turkey."[1] I waited for two years and ended up thousands of kilometers away from "home" to undertake the research for this book telling the stories of female directors from this country. And here I am, writing the first chapter of this journey. My story is intertwined with their stories and explored in the lines of this book. In our stories, we need to leave our homes, which I metaphorically describe as "drifting away." Indeed, the figure of the wandering, drifting woman who leaves home is a key character in Women's New Cinema of Turkey.

While following this drifting female figure (mostly diverting from the main paths, as drifting necessitates one do), I happened upon an essay by Tuna Erdem, one of the most influential film scholars from Turkey who is also a queer and feminist artist. In her article, she talks about her driftwood collection and describes the driftwood as such:

> When two words come together [drift and wood], we have a concept that almost has a story: wood pieces that snapped from the tree and were blown

> in the wind, that fell into the water and got caught in the current and reached the sea, that were washed ashore by the waves and got carved and polished by the mobile and feverish forces which they left themselves unarmored, stripped of their shells in all their haphazard wanderings. (Erdem 2019)

The story of the drifting wood is very similar to the story of the female figure that the contemporary female directors from Turkey insistently and repetitively construct in their narratives. Like driftwood, the female figure snaps away from her roots, her home, and her family and takes a journey. This snap, similar to Sara Ahmed's snap, is a "feminist snap," that is to be willing to "break ties that are damaging as well as to invest in new possibilities" (2017b, 162). This snapping is a willing, purposeful and intentional action; it is a decision to leave a damaging tie—the Angel—behind. That is how the snapping wood and the snapping female figure open themselves to new possibilities; their "haphazard wanderings." This "hap" in haphazard is a "queer hap," another Ahmed term (2010), because it is about subverting the common path and placing the hap—happenstance—in the story. So, the wanderings of the wood and the female figure are not sealed and congealed but they are willing to enter new, unknown paths. Leaving the shell that covers them, both the piece of wood and the female figure set out on journeys that transform them.

Understanding this "snap" as the first particularity of Women's New Cinema, in this chapter, I aim to explore the reasons for making the female figure leave and her transformation and self-reclamation along the way. For this, I will think through Sigmund Freud's concept of "uncanny." In his essay "The Uncanny" (1919), Freud draws attention to the fact that "*heimat*" (homeland), "*heimlich*" (familiar), "*unheimlich*" (uncanny) and "*geheim*" (secret) share the same root, "*heim*" (home). And interestingly, "*heimlich*," which means "native," "belonging to the home," "tame," and "friendly," also means "concealed," "behind someone's back," and "kept out of sight." That is how "*unheimlich*," which means "uneasy," "eerie," and "bloodcurdling," is both the antonym and synonym of "*heimlich*" (Freud 1919, 2–4). As noted by Julia Kristeva, with this word Freud:

> wanted to demonstrate at the outset, on the basis of a semantic study of the German adjective *heimlich* and its antonym *unheimlich*, that a negative meaning close to that of the antonym is already tied to the positive term *heimlich*, 'friendlily (sic) comfortable', which would also signify 'concealed, kept from sight', 'deceitful and malicious', 'behind someone's back'. Thus, in the very word *heimlich*, the familiar and intimate are reversed into their opposites, brought together with the contrary meaning of 'uncanny strangeness' harbored in *unheimlich*. (Kristeva 1991, 182)

I employed this term not because of its psychoanalytical connotations but because of the semantic game it includes. Like Freud, by focusing on the derivatives of "home," my aim is to understand the dynamics of the relationship between the female figure and her home, her family, city, country and their secrets. I also aim to explore the circumstances that make these spaces that are long known to her terrifying, dangerous and unfriendly. In other words, how do "*heim*"/"*heimat*" become "*unheimlich*," and how do unfamiliar, unknown spaces become the space of possibility for the women from Turkey imagined in the Women's New Cinema? Understanding the dynamics of the space for the female figure and the reasons she wants to leave them behind, I conceptualize outside, the "terrible beauty" (see Moten 2017; Hartman 2020) as the space of contemporary women's cinema in Turkey.

To reveal the relationship between the space and the female figure, I will analyze the film *Şimdiki Zaman/Present Tense* (Söylemez, 2012). I chose Mina, the protagonist of *Present Tense*, as the case study throughout this chapter because Mina's driftwood story provides meticulous details with which to conceptualize the space in women's films from Turkey: Mina feels insecure in her house, and she feels suffocated in her country.

Drifting From the House

To be able to explore the characteristics of home and its uncanny dynamics in Women's New Cinema, I want to delve into the secret nature of the word "uncanny." Freud states, "Why the usage of speech has extended *das Heimlich* into *das Unheimliche* for this uncanny is in reality nothing new or foreign, but something familiar and old" (1919, 13). He continues to define uncanny as "something which ought to have been kept concealed but which has nevertheless come to light" (1919, 13). In this book, "home" is defined as one of the most significant places in women's films from Turkey using these characteristics. In these films "home" can be imagined as the space of uncanny: when the family secrets that have been concealed come to light and the home, which has been something familiar for a very long time, becomes uncanny. The uncanny dynamics of "*heim*" are explored in more detail with the help of *Present Tense*, Mina's driftwood story.

Present Tense is the first fiction feature film directed by Belmin Söylemez. It tells the story of Mina, a twenty-eight-year-old university graduate who has been unemployed for a long time. Mina has problematic ties with her family, she wants to move on from her divorce and she must leave her apartment in a month as it is going to be turned into a hotel. Mina wants to leave Turkey but she is unemployed and broke. To immigrate to the USA, Mina needs to find money and get a visa, so she starts working as a fortune teller in a café in Beyoğlu, a main district of Istanbul (Figure 1.1).

It is ambiguous whether she reads the fortunes she tells in the coffee cups or if all of the women she sees have similar fortunes. In the meantime, Fazi, the other fortune teller in the café, wants to be friends with Mina, and she even dreams of the two of them opening a café together. Tayfun, the owner of the café, hopes to find the love he seeks in Mina. But Mina neither wants to own a café nor be someone's lover. She just wants to get away. Söylemez leaves her film open-ended; the end of the film shows images of several coffee cups, indicating several future possibilities.

The first scene of *Present Tense* shows Mina's face while a man's voice says, "Do not smile. Do not sulk. Tuck your hair behind your ears. Lean your head. Look across."[2] As is understood from the instructions, she is getting her passport photo taken. In the next scene, we see some busts of men and Mina sitting on a bench in a park. She then finds a phone booth and rings several numbers to apply for jobs but gets rejected from all of them. All these images, instructions, and rules along with the busts of male leaders who established Turkish states throughout history make it obvious that Mina is surrounded; these images "become a spatial image of the tyrannical world that oppresses Mina" (Çiçekoğlu 2015, 109). Walking a narrow path surrounded by wire fences, Mina arrives the street where her house is.

Figure 1.1 Mina reads women's fortunes in coffee cups. A still from *Present Tense*.

Furniture is piled up on the pavement outside Mina's apartment block and Mina understands that one of the tenants is moving out. Soon, it is revealed that this makes Mina the last tenant of the building, which is going to be turned into a hotel. Mina enters the apartment building and climbs a few stairs; the damaged plaster walls tell us how old and weary the apartment is. We then see the tenant leaving (Figures 1.2 and 1.3). As Çiçekoğlu states (2015, 110), these images suggest that Mina also "gets disconnected" from this apartment, her home.

Mina enters her apartment, which is poorly decorated. There is almost nothing personal that makes this apartment Mina's house; there are no family

Figure 1.2 Mina watches her neighbor moving out. A still from *Present Tense*.

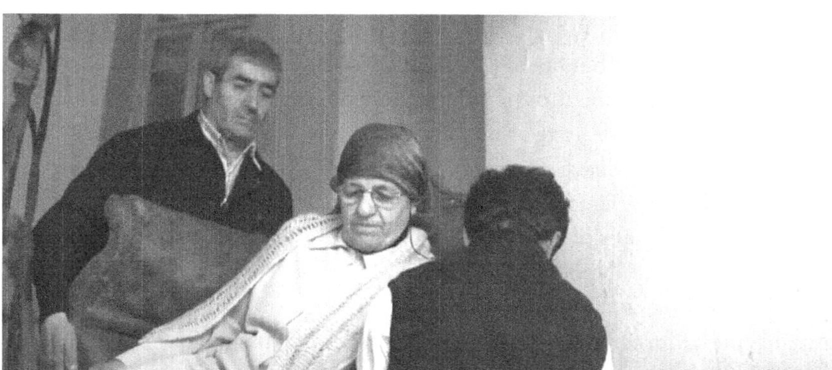

Figure 1.3 From Mina's gaze, her neighbor. A still from *Present Tense*.

photos on the walls, no family heirlooms around. Like Mina, the house is lonely and empty. She has a small TV, a sofa and torn, thin, transparent curtains that are powerless to hide the inside from the outside. Neither the curtains nor the walls of this apartment give Mina the feeling of security. Ironically, the house becomes less secure when the hotel management sends a security guard to the building. Mina hears this man's footsteps on the stairs and has nightmares in which he enters her house. She hides the dollars she is saving to go to the USA inside a box that she puts inside the wardrobe of the room she sleeps in, but she often counts the money as if to check that no one has taken any when she is not around. The strange feeling released from the house, which is supposed to be safe, familiar, and friendly, turns the atmosphere uncanny. This uncanny feeling of the house is very similar to the uncanny feeling Turkey gives to its citizens; in this regard, her house is representative of both Mina and the entire country, with its lonely citizens who expect something horrible will happen to them at any time.

There is another house depicted in Mina's story. Mina is invited by one of her customers to a house gathering where women come together and pay Mina to read their fortune from coffee cups (Figure 1.4). We see lots of food and lots of women chatting to each other. It is clearly a family house; we see family furniture and happy family photos with faces crowded together in the frames. After all, does family not mean to be happy and to gather together in that happiness? It does not for these women, who seem to be unhappy and lonely. Mina reads one woman's fortune:

> I should tell you one thing; you behave too well to this man. You dance to his tune. If he loves you one time, you love him three times. And I am seeing a thing within a thing. There is this house and there is this other house. He goes from one house to the other but he's neither here nor there.

With the secret about her husband coming to light, the woman starts to cry.

The man we hear about but do not see is the husband cheating on his wife. He can neither stay nor leave or he can both stay and leave simultaneously. Will the woman be able to leave one day? Will she dare to "spoil" the happiness of her family by refusing to construct a pretense of happiness? Or does Mina read her own life from the lines of the coffee? Did she get divorced because she stopped pretending she was happy within her family? Does Mina always tell her own story when she reads the cups or do all women have similar houses, similar families and similar fortunes? The film narrative does not answer these questions.

In addition to these houses, we get also engage with Mina's "father's home" (the family home is called the father's home in Turkish) in a phone conversation

Figure 1.4 Mina reads women's fortunes. A still from *Present Tense*.

Mina has with her sister. Mina calls her sister to ask her if she can provide her with the official papers she needs to apply for a US visa. When her sister answers the phone, we understand that she does not recognize Mina's number, which suggests how estranged they are. Mina anxiously says she needs her sister's help and asks if she can sign the papers. In return, her sister asks if Mina has called someone. This someone is probably their mother or the father Mina refuses to talk to. The old issues unfold and Mina realizes that her sister will not help but will only continue to judge her. She hangs up the phone and throws it on the floor. She looks outside and cries (Figure 1.5). It is obvious that Mina cannot satisfy the expectations of her family and cannot meet the requirements her familial relationships necessitate.

Turkish academic and author Asuman Suner says, "Home is impossible. The houses in which we grew up become unbearable, even the slightest feeling of taking shelter under the family roof messes with the musty smell of family interests" (2006a, 317). This is how Mina relates to her sister. Later in the film, we learn another family secret: Mina's aunt immigrated to the USA because the family wanted her to get married while she was still studying and no one has heard from her since she left Turkey. Is this why Mina stopped communicating with her family as well? Is Mina's family judgmental and conditional because Mina wants to leave them as her aunt did? After all, "to destroy the 'family' may be experienced as worse than murder or more selfish than suicide" (Laing 1971, 14).

Figure 1.5 Mina's view from her torn curtain. A still from *Present Tense.*

In the beginning of *Anna Karenina*, Tolstoy writes, "Happy families are all alike; every unhappy family is unhappy in its own way" ([1875–7] 1985, 13). But there is a certain taste of unhappiness in the heavy, suffocating air of the working-class houses in Turkey. That is what is sensed in Mina's family home. The female literary critic Nurdan Gürbilek describes these working-class houses as follows:

> Taps drip constantly in these houses. Metal containers are placed under the taps, the water makes a monotonous sound as it drips into the vessel, the vessels fill, the water overflows, leaving a stubborn yellow rust mark where it overflows. Again, in these houses, old and unused items are not thrown away, they are kept; punctured pots, cups with broken handles, shrunken clothes, old buttons, wool ripped from old sweaters. In this pile of items, there are always a few rare items hidden from the children: a couple of bottles of whiskey, which are kept waiting to be served to the right guests, waiting in a secret corner of the house because the right guest never arrives. (2019, 66–7)

Writing about Mina's family home, I could very well be describing my own. I am revealing the secrets of my family house because it has a profound effect on my own filmmaking. It was a working-class home located at the top of a hill. It had the same guest room waiting for the right guest to come who never arrives, the ceramic plate bearing the image of Mustafa Kemal Atatürk[3] hung on the wall proving my father's dedication to authority, the closed curtains in the bright daylight hiding the inside from the outside reflecting my mother's paranoia, the yellow walls and the boredom, uneasiness, unhappiness lingering in the air. "There are houses that I want to disagree with; houses, carpets, songs, teachers . . . There are rules I want to disagree with" (Özlü 1994, 12). All these closed curtains and cold guest rooms turning our houses into uncanny spaces make us want to go; we want to kill the Angels in these houses and break from our relationships and family ties.

Gül Yaşartürk explains that in Turkey, "the films produced in the 2000s are films in which the institution of the family is perhaps more seriously criticized than it has ever been" (2014, 2). It is not a coincidence that most of the films she mentions in her essay belong to Women's New Cinema. In the films of contemporary female filmmakers from Turkey, the house and the family, which are familiar and supposed to be friendly, are the sources of the uncanny. This is in sharp contrast to Yeşilçam films, where the evil comes to the family from outside and it is eliminated by the resistance of the family by holding on to each other. In Women's New Cinema it is the father who abuses his children in *Atlıkarınca/Merry-Go-Round* (Başarır, 2011); it is the husband who rapes his wife in *Tereddüt/Clair Obscur* (Ustaoğlu, 2016); it is the mother who abuses her children in *Köksüz/Nobody's Home* (Akçay, 2014) and *Anayurdu/Motherland* (Tüzen, 2015); it is the daughters who cannot help their mother when she becomes sick in *Pandora'nın Kutusu/Pandora's Box* (Ustaoğlu, 2008); it is the mother who leaves her daughter behind in *Ez Firiyam Tu Mayi Li Cih/I Flew You Stayed* (Arslan, 2012). Home is seen as the most dangerous place for a woman as observed by the contemporary female filmmakers of Women's New Cinema. These directors can be evaluated as part of the continuum of the long genealogy of feminist filmmakers reflecting the danger of the family house in women-oriented genres like melodrama and Gothic tales.[4]

Contemporary female filmmakers from Turkey create a new dynamic between the family houses and the female characters. If I adapt Nurdan Gürbilek's comments (2020, 73–4) on one of the early formulations of Gilles Deleuze's "line of flight,"[5] I say that in Women's New Cinema, the problem is not to be free from the mother but to find a way out in a world where the mother herself cannot find a way out. Not only to get rid of the mother's house but to go out of a whole representation system integrated with the mother's house. In this sense, the female characters of Women's New Cinema not only attempt to rescue themselves from the moldy family ties but also from the entire system constraining their freedom. It is also about giving up the trial to save the mother from that world understanding that everyone needs to kill her own Angel to find her way out. Similarly, the line of flight drawn by Women's

New Cinema provides its audience with representations that can be a lifeline, but these representations are not a rescue effort.[6]

Women's New Cinema allows a site for the secrets of our houses to become more visible through facing them and recognizing them. In *The Play* (Esmer, 2005), the female figures confront the patriarchal codes of society; in *Geriye Kalan/What Remains* (Vitrinel, 2012), the audience questions morality over the story of a family; in *Hayatboyu/Lifelong* (Özge, 2013), the female figure confronts herself through the secrets of her family; in *Merry-Go-Round*, the female figure investigates the secrets of her family; in *Nefesim Kesilene Kadar/Until I Lose My Breath* (Balcı, 2015), the female figure reveals the secrets of her father; in *Toz Bezi/Dust Cloth* (Öztürk, 2015), the female figures face her family and the society; in Zefir/*Zephyr* (Baş, 2010) and *Nobody's Home*, the female figures confront their own motherhood. Contemporary female directors, through these stories, unfold the secrets of Turkish society.

The confrontation in these films is the act of burning down the house. While women's fantasies about literally burning down their fathers' houses appear quite frequently in bildungsroman novels by female authors from Turkey,[7] I use "burning down" as a metaphor for destroying a space that is supposed to be safe but which in fact is uncanny and entraps women. Like Mina, the female figure of Women's New Cinema destroys the house by revealing its secrets and leaves familial ties behind to start her own journey. On this new road, the space of the unfamiliar and unknown becomes friendly because despite it being somewhere that is not home—the unhomely—it enables her to transform into the one who she is willing to be. Then when we as women from Turkey decide to snap or, if we already have, that Women's New Cinema has a space without a roof can provide us with a feminist shelter.

The Space of Women's New Cinema: "Terrible Beauty"[8]

The female figure of Women's New Cinema has a different relationship with the home as well as outside the home. Unlike the female figure in Turkish films of the previous decade, she leaves home and her domestic dreams behind to have her own experience outside. Her being in a public space changes the dynamics of the space as well as proving the well-known fact that the city of Istanbul is losing its unique façade to gentrification. That is why in this section, I consider the connection between Mina and the streets of Istanbul together with other films of Women's New Cinema. The former only reveals the story of the streets belonging to the city but Women's New Cinema also hosts the stories of streets belonging to the town.

Turkish filmmakers have produced films located in urban cities and rural towns since the 1930s, but the meaning of urban spaces has changed drastically over the years with the changing sociocultural and political landscape of Turkey. While these early-day films tell the stories of people living in their rural towns, the films that were produced in the 1960s started narrating the difficult conditions of the migrants who moved from eastern rural towns to western urban cities. After the 1980s coup, the number of films set in rural towns increased and they told the stories of people who had returned from the big city, immigrating back to their rural towns (Erdoğan 2019, 42–9).

As "the town" is depicted as a place one immigrates from in these films, the city, which is nearly always Istanbul, is depicted as the place those immigrants arrive at. This scene of arrival is remarkably similar across films, from *Gurbet Kuşları/Birds of Exile* (Refiğ, 1964) to *Gelin/The Bride* (Akad, 1973) and *Bitmeyen Yol/The Road That Has No End* (Sağıroğlu, 1965); characters arrive in Istanbul at Haydarpaşa train station with wooden luggage in their hands. They look at the vastness and beauty of the city, the seagulls in the blue sky, and the light twinkling on the sea that represent high hopes and the great opportunities waiting for the newcomers.

But the promises of the city may fade away within a couple of decades as the newcomers face psychological problems, economic hardships, cultural and moral degradation, and isolation (Alkan 2014, 270). They rage against the city as they do not belong there and instead create their own towns within Istanbul (Barış 2010, 281). That is why in the new wave films of the 2000s, the city is no longer a "paradise on earth" but "a source of terror": it is depressing, suffocating, unrestful and jammed, a trap people want to get out of (Çiçekoğlu 2015, 72). We see the same suffocating city silhouette in Mina's story. The moment she steps out of her lonely house, it is the gray city, the boredom of the city that surrounds her.

Istanbul is not only a background element in Mina's journey but the city also plays a character within the film. Indeed, the story of the city is entangled with Mina's story. In the last twenty or thirty years, Istanbul has become a giant construction site, losing its unique façade as the city's distinctive features are transformed into the generic type of buildings seen in cities all over the world. It has no connection with its history and we do not have such a city in our memory. One of the reasons Mina's state is precarious is because she loses her house to gentrification, which is happening with many of the historic buildings in the city. Söylemez explains that this is where the line between reality and fiction blurs:

> When we were filming Mina's house in Yeldeğirmeni, we wrote it as an evacuated building that will be a hotel in the script. When we went there again two months or one month after the shooting, we saw that it was sealed and then it was turned into a hotel. So, these changes happen in the blink of an eye. It

> is unbelievable. That's why, through the eyes of a person walking, a woman walking, a walking person, Istanbul becomes a city that makes you feel sad all the time. (Söylemez quoted in Fontini 2020; personal communication)[9]

There is a similar connection between the city and the female figure in *Kaygı/Inflame* (Özçelik, 2017). The female protagonist of the film, Hasret, tries to unveil the truth hidden deep in her memory as the city constantly changes in the background due to gentrification. The more Hasret walks through the streets of Istanbul trying to remember her past, the more ruins we see from the city, leading us to slowly forget its previous façade. There is a parallel between the loss of Hasret's personal memory and the loss of our collective memory that the "old" Istanbul belongs to. Like Hasret, who does not remember her own past, we are losing the present; the fading image of the city becomes visible in Hasret's walks.

In this country, we experience something new every day; every day a woman gets murdered, a peaceful protest is attacked, a historic building is torn down, and an old cinematheque is turned into a shopping mall. And we forget. With the transformation of that place, all our memories, our laughter there, the conversations we had with friends, everything changes and transforms in an instant. It is as if they erase our pasts in an instant. It is as if they erase us.

It is the same gray image of Istanbul in *Present Tense*, emphasizing the non-belonging of Mina to the city. As the male character of the film, Tayfun, asks, "What does Mina do there," in that city? There is a relationship between the transformation of the city and the alienation of Mina. The frame within a frame of Mina in Istanbul reveals a claustrophobic feeling. As described by Çiçekoğlu,

> While looking out the window, walking down a street that leads down to the sea, feeling overwhelmed at the numbered desk of the internet café, waiting for the visa form to come out of the printer, trying to fill out the form in front of the kitchen window in her house, we internalize Mina's desire to escape from this city. (2015, 111)

If the female figure of Women's New Cinema deals with the boredom of the city, how does she relate to the town? As mentioned earlier, the relationship between the protagonist and town has changed over the years. The new wave films that take place in towns have two different inclinations. Some films narrate the town as "a place of happiness," while others see the town as "a dark and secluded place inhabited by people who are fearful, prone to violence, and dislike each other" (Algan 2010, 140). Town functions in the same way in Women's New Cinema. Films such as *The Play* and *Kraliçe Lear/Queen Lear* (Esmer, 2019) describe the town from inside and narrate it as the place of happiness whereas films like

Nobody's Home, *Motherland*, *Clair Obscur*, and *Zephyr* approach town critically and associate it with darkness.

Regardless of whether she lives in the town or the city, the female figure in Women's New Cinema has a troublesome relationship with the outside because of a contradiction: whether the space is a source of freedom or boredom. With Mina, for instance, on one hand we feel the sense of boredom released from the gray city through her observing gaze, while on the other we feel a sense of freedom through her haphazard wanderings. She aimlessly walks the streets of Istanbul; she does not have a destination to aim for or someone to catch.[10]

Cultural studies have highlighted the relationship between the city and women since the 1980s and focused on the women who take the streets as their place and wander in the public space freely (Çiçekoğlu 2007, 81). Janet Wolff, one of the academics contributing to this discourse, writes:

> The problem is, though, that it is also the literature of modernity which has been impoverished by ignoring the lives of women. The dandy, the *flaneur*, the hero, the stranger—all figures invoked to epitomize the experience of modern life—are invariably male figures. In 1831, when George Sand wanted to experience Paris life and to learn about the ideas and arts of her time, she dressed as a boy, to give herself the freedom she knew women could not share . . . The disguise made the life of the *flaneur* available to her; as she knew very well, she could not adopt the non-existent role of *flaneuse*. Women could not stroll alone in the city. (Wolff 2004, 9; original emphasis)

Both Wolff (2004, 9) and Elisabeth Wilson (1991, 8) argue that women cannot wander in the city freely; Wilson writes, "to be a woman—an individual, not part of a family or kin group—in the city, is to become a prostitute—a public woman" (1991, 8). The cinema of Turkey has many female characters confirming this point. Sabiha, the female figure in *Vesikalı Yarim/My Prostitute Love* (Akad, 1968); Nesibe, the female figure in *Benim Sinemalarım/My Cinemas* (Füruzan and Karamustafa, 1990); and Rosa, the female protagonist in *Seni Seviyorum Rosa/ Rosa, I Love You* (Özgentürk, 1992) are all depicted as wanderers and prostitutes. But the wandering female figure of Women's New Cinema is not a prostitute; she is not saved by the male character and she does not drag him to catastrophe.

In her book *Flâneuse*, Lauren Elkin writes,

> Space is not neutral. Space is a feminist issue. The space we occupy—here in the city, we city dwellers—is constantly remade and unmade, constructed and wondered at. "Space is a doubt," wrote Georges Perec; "I have constantly to mark it, to designate it. It's never mine, never given to me, I have to conquer it." (2017, 416)

The space conquered by women on screen and in reality is a feminist issue. Women in Turkey occupy the streets of the city by having a life there. The backstreets of Istanbul are inhabited by us; single women, Syrian refugees, street artists, sex workers, faggots, working-class Kurds, and Blacks.[11] To the eye of a Westerner or of a bourgeois, these little ghettos in Beyoğlu, Tarlabaşı, and Tophane might seem exotic or ugly, but we claim this "terrible beauty" (see Hartman 2020). Despite the terror and violence, there is joy. Women toast their glasses of rakı at a tavern in Karaköy while two men kiss each other at a dark corner in Gezi Park. Death and constant life-making . . . Fred Moten says, "it hurts so much that we have to celebrate. That we have to celebrate is what hurts so much" (2017, xiii) . . . This is how we manage to refuse the unlivability of our own country.

The uncanny corners of Istanbul, this terrible beauty also transforms us; it enables us to become someone new. While walking haphazardly, Mina finds a job at a café where she meets Fazi and Tayfun. They start wandering the streets of Istanbul together. This is how Mina keeps dreaming of another possibility. Like Mina, the female figure in *Inflame*, Hasret, walks aimlessly in the streets of the city. Her haphazard wanderings make her open to new possibilities and new happenings. The dog she encounters in the park, the newspaper headlines she sees at the buffet, and the news she watches in the restaurant she happens to enter help her recall her childhood memories. Outside, the "space of happenstance" enables her to become someone else, someone who owns her past.

Women occupying public space also changes the dynamics of the space. For instance, the village women in *The Play* intervene with the flow of everyday life through their haphazard wanderings in the streets of their villages. Upon preparing a theatre play that narrates their private life, the village women walk into their village to invite their husbands, their neighbors and the village people to their play (Figure 1.6). In *Queen Lear,* the same women perform Shakespeare's play *King Lear* (1606) and again they wander around in villages to invite the villagers to their play. These wanderings make their existence and their performance visible to the villagers. Their claiming of public space transforms society, their families and themselves. Zeynep, one of the theatre players, says to her husband, "Mustafa, I am not the one I used to be. Many things have changed."

In Women's New Cinema, the city is surrounded and its familiar façade is fading away. But at the same time, outside is the "space of happenstance" for the female figure. This space is supposed to be unfamiliar but turns into a friendly space where the female figure wanders haphazardly. Her being out of the house, being on the way to somewhere else and experiencing freedom help her to confront herself, to change, to transform. In Giuliana Bruno's terms (2018), she

Figure 1.6 Arslanköy village-women theatre group walks in the streets of a town. A still from *Queen Lear*.

turns into a "voyageur" who actively experiences the things rather than staying a "voyeur," passively watching the things happen. In this way I understand outside/our terrible beauty, the unknown space full of possibility or the space where her story begins, as the space of Women's New Cinema.

"Turkey, You Ate Me!"[12]

Turkish poet Ahmet Hamdi Tanpınar wrote, "Turkey does not give the opportunity to its children to be busy with anything other than itself. In this respect, it looks very much like our house" (2013, 259). Living in Turkey does feel like living in a home with an authoritarian father who does not allow his children to enjoy their lives. In this section, this resemblance—the resemblance between "*heim*" (home) and "*heimat*" (homeland) and their connection with "*geheim*" (secret)—is examined.

"If you had the opportunity, you wouldn't stay here for a minute," says Mina, reading the coffee cup of one of her customers. She continues:

> There's something you've been wanting to do for years. It looks like a journey. Somewhere overseas. It's like the end of the road is closed. Something feels missing. I see a ship. Three quarters of this ship is visible. It's stuck on something on a ledge, as if it was stranded. If the ship gets rid of it, it will open and go.

If Mina had the opportunity, she would not stay in Turkey "for a minute." But she is surrounded by rules, instructions and forms full of difficult questions stranding her there. Mina does not have a secure job, she does not have an address to stay in the USA, she does not have papers documenting the wealth of her family. "To go out" of Turkey means "to be able to go" if you are its citizen and Mina is not "eligible" to leave the country. But Mina continues; she continues to imagine another possibility for herself even when no one around her believes. Her resilience is a rejection, she rejects the unlivability of her current environment. Like Mina, Women's New Cinema persists. In such a misogynistic atmosphere, their continuously making films is a stubborn act and a resistance to the cruelty of now.

Mina continues reading the coffee lines:

> You've been hiding here for a while. But now you've decided. But there are obstacles in front of you, as if a cloud of fog has covered your life. You're saying what am I doing here? You surprise yourself. You're saying, "Is this really me?"

Söylemez created Mina as a young woman who wants to leave her country because this female figure has many connections with her own self and the women she knows:

> The movie has a lot to do with me, and the young women I know, from the very beginning. That's why, it's mostly the story of young women. There were themes such as the fact that I wanted to go, my friends wanted to go, the periods of unemployment we experienced, lack of belonging, looking for an exit, and not being able to fully belong here. And a young urban woman's quest for freedom, the desire to start all over again, the desire to leave everything behind, that is, to leave behind everything on which she is dependent . . . Of course, generations have changed, years have changed, but the desire to go has always remained. (Fontini, personal communication; 2020)

The desire to go away from Turkey has always remained—at a certain point, nearly everybody wanted to leave the country. I was one of those people. And I went. Because we were so stuck in Turkey that we could hardly live. Young people, queer people, women, dissidents and minorities were in a state of unhappiness; there was despair in the air. The atmosphere of the country has gotten worse since then. Every one of us knows what causes this unhappiness.

The construction of space in Women's New Cinema not only reflects the experience of being a woman but also reflects the experience of being a woman under the ongoing political tension in Turkey. Ceylan Özgün Özçelik summarizes the atmosphere of Turkey and of her film *Inflame*:

> The film's atmosphere [an atmosphere of fear] is suffocating, as it has been for the last few years in Turkey. It's the paranoia that, at any second, someone might come to your house and take you "somewhere" and you'll be inside a prison without knowing what your fault is. [Even] without a crime being proven, you can be punished for years. It can be just because of a Twitter post or a talk or signing a petition. Every hour something was happening, it is not possible for the Westerners to understand. It's a unique feeling for Middle Eastern lands nowadays that there might be a war starting in the morning and a coup attempt the same night. A civil disobedience and state of emergency. Media publications have been closed down, 2,000 academics have been fired, government officials have been on hold, fired. Day to day, everything changed. The Kurdish situation, nothing left. Social media has been stopped. All the media available are speaking from one main centre, not hiding that they are saying the same thing. Seven newspapers had the exact headline. (Berlinale Talents 2017)

Seven newspapers had the same headline both in the fictitious world Özçelik created and in Turkish reality.

The atmosphere of fear, a concept often used nowadays to describe the uncanny feeling of Turkey, is directly connected with "the quest for a father as absolute authority" (Parla 2019, 260). It is the uneasiness that grows the quest. It is an uneasiness released by "the father" to grow the quest. This quest can be described as "the willingness to escape from freedom, the insecurity when faced with the possibility of a fatherless vacuum, and the need to fill it at all costs" (2019, 260). This quest has continued to inform Turkish thought for decades.

This father of absolute authority, the President of the Republic of Turkey, has in the last two decades created a "new Turkey" that now identifies itself with neoliberal Islamic codes rather than the codes of a secular state. This cracked the nation into two: "The Talking Turkey and The Silent One" (Gürbilek 2020, 49). Gürbilek cites Tülin Ural's essay on "native and national secrets" and describes the Silent Turkey as the one "keeping the secrets of the 'family'" (2020, 49). The "native and national" discourse put into use by the "father" strengthens the bonds and the sensation of belonging to a family. Gürbilek states, "Those who come from the same 'native and national' family know the secret just because they come from the same family. The fact that they know this shows that they are native and national" (2020, 49). Or, in other words "being 'native and national' means knowing where to talk and where to be silent" (2020, 49).

Gezi Park Protests (the largest grassroots resistance in the history of Turkey),[13] and the films of contemporary female directors show us that the relationship of women with the father, state and country is quite different. It is a willingness to seek freedom, to reject the father's authority. It is a refusal to know where to talk and where to stay silent; it is about talking or "leaking" the native and national secrets of the family. It is a leak because it breaks the code of being a member of a family which requires keeping family secrets within the family, and it also breaks the code of belonging to a nation which requires keeping national secrets within the nation.[14]

Women's New Cinema rejects the codes of "normal" morality and instead embraces the feminist ethics of responsibility. This is to "risk exposing that which the culture wants silenced" (Citron 1999, 273), to question the normative order. By constructing female images as social and historical therefore reflecting the sociodemographic reality of Turkey, Women's New Cinema reveals the "secrets" of the country. The contemporary female filmmakers from Turkey accept the challenge to review Turkish culture, society, and history from the perspective of "others," that is women's personal stories. While reviewing our own history is a form of responsibility, telling the stories of "others" that have never been told is a political act. Women's filmmaking in Turkey claims alterity as a form of resistance. Being personal and political and accepting personal and collective responsibility simultaneously, Women's New Cinema adapts a new ethical standpoint: neither the family nor the country is sacred; nothing needs to be kept secret, and all voices must be heard.[15]

The weaknesses of Turkish society are being narrated through the secrets of the unhappy families, as seen in the following films. for example: *Zephyr, Nobody's Home, I Flew You Stayed, Clair Obscur, Lifelong, What Remains, Merry-Go-Round,* and *Until I Lose My Breath*. The national secrets are told through the personal stories of the main characters in *İki Tutam Saç: Dersim'in Kayıp Kızları/Two Locks of Hair: The Lost Girls of Dersim* (Gündoğan, 2010), *Hay Way Zaman: Dersim'in Kayıp Kızları/Unburied in The Past—The Missing Girls of The Dersim* (Gündoğan, 2014), *Nahide'nin Türküsü/Hush!* (Baş, 2009), and *Güneşe Yolculuk/Journey to the Sun* (Ustaoğlu, 1999), while the narrative of *Inflame* allows for discussion about the lies of the media and the authoritarian state and the female character of *Bulutları Beklerken/Waiting for the Clouds* (Ustaoğlu, 2003) reveals the effects of the monocultural politics of the Turkish state. It is not a coincidence that in all these films, it is the female figure who breaks from the ties that damage her. As Gürbilek suggests, "The irreparability of being forcibly taken away from home . . . And the pleasure of being away from home . . . Loss or opportunity?" (2020, 22).

Conclusion: "The Subject of Revolution is Ourselves, is Our Lives"[16]

As argued in this chapter, the female figures of Women's New Cinema want to go, go, go, go—from the family fathers in pajamas, from their husbands, from their children, and from the Angels in their houses. Like driftwood, she snaps from home, from her old self. In *Present Tense*, Mina wants to leave Turkey, a place that hinders her from realizing herself; in *Nobody's Home*, Feride wants to go away from her family home, to leave her mother; in *Clair Obscur*, Şehnaz leaves her husband who discourages her from enjoying her life; in *Waiting for the Clouds*, Ayşe/Eleni leaves Turkey, a country that oppresses her identity, to Greece so she is able to reclaim herself; in *Zephyr*, Ay wants to leave the town, although it means leaving her daughter behind; in *Motherland*, Nesrin leaves city life to be able to stay on her own and start writing; in *Ben ve Nuri Bala/Me and Nuri Bala* (Önel, 2009), Esmeray leaves her hometown so she can realize herself as a transexual artist; in *I Flew You Stayed*, Arslan leaves her village and country to be able to understand her roots, to unveil the secrets of her family and Turkey; in *Dust Cloth*, Nesrin leaves her daughter behind to embrace her new life alone. Producing narratives in which the female figure snaps from such bonds is an essential intervention to the ongoing patriarchal tradition. It is also a quest to experience unprecedented freedom: snapping from a familial bond means being able to snap from any bond, or in other words, "to break with the family is to risk breaking everything up" (Laing 1971, 13). Women's New Cinema, in this sense, is a reminder. Of this risk, of this possibility.

After snapping from the tree, the driftwood is blown in the wind, falls into the water and gets caught in the current. In a similar way, the female figure of Women's New Cinema happens upon others during her haphazard wanderings. Mina comes across the realities of her family and her country; Feride, Nesrin, and Mizgin Müjde see the reality of their mothers; Şehnaz faces the reality of her husband; Ayşe/Eleni meets the realities of this society, her family, and this country . . . The list can continue endlessly.

We need to heal because, as Audre Lorde says, "We have been nurtured in a sick, abnormal society" (2017a, 4). Healing can come from "the process of reclaiming ourselves as well as the terms of that society" (2017a, 4). This is how the female figure of Women's New Cinema connects to herself and her abnormal society. By opening the "interior" spaces to the public, she reveals the secrets of the country and her family. She then leaves these damaging ties behind. It is not only about breaking free from the father, from the mother, from the husband, it is also about starting a journey. Similar to driftwood, the female figure starts wandering outside freely and undergoes a transformation through the confrontations she has in the "terrible beauty". In *Clair Obscur*, *Waiting for the Clouds*, *Inflame*, *What Remains*, *The Play*, *Queen Lear*, *Lifelong*, *Until I Lose My Breath*, *Dust Cloth*, *Me and Nuri Bala*, and *İşe Yarar Bir Şey/Something Useful* (Esmer, 2017), we watch female characters transforming into someone else, someone new. In all these films, the subject of the revolution is the woman herself; not her child, not her mother, not her country. The female directors of Women's New Cinema reclaim the terms of this society by constructing such characters. Cinema is the remedy, the resistance helping them handle the present time, the nightmare of history.

Women's New Cinema invites the viewer to witness the female figure's experience, to inhabit her house and to see the country through her gaze. This figure appears insecure inside the house; she appears alone in the city. The viewer witnesses her desire to leave, they might even desire her to leave. They watch her remember or, as Özçelik suggests, "A woman remembers, so will the others" (Özçelik quoted in Aytaç and Çiftçi 2017, 29). By inviting the viewer to understand her story, one in which she must find a way out, the directors invite us to see that it is possible to snap. Women's New Cinema is about taking the possibility of leaving the Angel behind. The door of the house opens to the streets of terrible beauty where we can meet the new person we turn into while walking there haphazardly.

Notes

1. I discuss the particularities of this new Turkey in the third section of this chapter, titled "Turkey, You Ate Me!"
2. This quote and all other film quotes in this book have been translated from Turkish to English by me.
3. Mustafa Kemal Atatürk was the first president of Turkey.
4. I would like to thank Dr. Janice Loreck for drawing my attention to this point.
5. According to Deleuze, the major institutions like family, occupation, military service, school determine certain paths for the individual. The line of flight subverts this identified path and enables the individual to become something else than they are programmed to be (Deleuze and Parnet 1990, 74–169).
6. Here, I borrowed the words used by Sarah Franklin (2017) describing the work of Sara Ahmed.
7. Burning the house down or having the fantasy of burning the house down is also a common finale of the bildungsroman novels written by many female authors from Turkey such as Sevgi Soysal, Adalet Ağaoğlu, Leyla Erbil, Latife Tekin, Füruzan, and Aslı Erdoğan. Similar to the major concern of these bildungsroman novels, the major concern of this chapter is to understand how female characters dare to take their own lives into their own hands. It is not a coincidence that the female characters of the novels and films are created by women artists from Turkey.

8. I borrow the concept "terrible beauty" from Fred Moten (2017) and Saidiya Hartman (2020).
9. The interviews have been translated from Turkish to English by Kübra Kelebekoğlu.
10. These particularities of the female figure fit with the characteristics of the "*flâneuse*." The term "*flâneur*" is traditionally assigned to men but "*flâneuse*" defines women wandering aimlessly in the city. But, the conditions experienced by the female figure of Women's New Cinema make it impossible for her to wander the city in a carefree way because she is too occupied with the trouble of being a woman under the ongoing sociopolitical tension of Turkey. That is why I do not employ the term "*flâneuse*" to define her.
11. See Orhan Atasoy's song, "Gemiler" (Atasoy 1992) to have a short visit to this terrible beauty.
12. This subtitle is a reference to a line Ahmet Hamdi Tanpınar (2013) wrote in his diary.
13. See "Meet Me in the Evening for a Kiss in Taksim Square" (Fontini 2022a) to explore the details of Gezi protest.
14. To understand the relationship between feminism and "leaking," see Sara Ahmed's lecture "Complaint as Feminist Pedagogy" (2021), which is published on her blog feministkilljoys.
15. Here, I adapted some of the particularities of the new Israeli (feminist) documentary (Munk 2011) to my context.
16. I borrowed this sentence from Audre Lorde (2017a, 4).

Chapter 2

Companions of Nesibe: Female Representation in Women's New Cinema

It was an afternoon in July of 2017. The meeting I had been anticipating for months was finally taking place. I was at Pera Palace, Beyoğlu with author–director Füruzan. She talked about the consciousness of the 1960s world, the cultural life of Berlin and *Papirüs* magazine. She then started talking about Nesibe, the female protagonist of her film *My Cinemas*. Nesibe, who states the hypocrisy of her family and the society out loud, is to me the strongest feminist character in the cinema of Turkey. Füruzan said, "What she [Nesibe] experiences is painful not pitiful, there is a difference" (Füruzan quoted in Fontini 2020, 149). The discussions I carry into this chapter are born from this sentiment.

As women from Turkey, our collective journeys and the stories we create tend to be painful by nature because of the geography in which we happen to exist. It is always one step away; from pain to pity, sadness to arabesque, trouble to "save me." The directors of Yeşilçam melodramas and the directors of arabesque noir cinema[1] mostly choose to construct highly dramatic narratives featuring female images who try to find solutions through men; they create destitute womanhood. However, the contemporary female directors of Women's New Cinema create a world where the audience can look at women from Turkey with new eyes. These directors portray complex female characters and their multiple experiences in narratives where the female characters occupy the subject position. To analyze this characteristic of Women's New Cinema, this chapter focuses on the diverse female subjectivities and the agency of female characters. Exploring the representation and characterization of female characters, the chapter also challenges Asuman Suner (2006a, 47), who defines the female figures of New Cinema as "Vasfiye's sisters"[2] and claims that the stories of the new wave films are based on the "absence of women" and that the narrative unfolds through their silence. The chapter concludes that, despite having painful (but not pitiful) lives, the female characters of Women's New Cinema are companions of Nesibe.

The title of this chapter, "Companions of Nesibe," argues that the female protagonists in Women's New Cinema are the indicators of a new era in the cinematic landscape of Turkey and their active presence voices an extensive sociopolitical criticism of the current atmosphere. Their subjectivity functions as a tool of resistance. The increasingly authoritarian regime in Turkey also changed the culture into an authoritarian one. The freedom of expression, especially the voices of women, queer people, religious minorities, and Kurds, is greatly restricted and opposing views are marginalized. This chapter argues that in such an atmosphere contemporary female filmmakers reject the roles assigned to women by making their voices heard. The active subjectivity of female characters challenges women's subordination within oppressive forms.

Firstly, to be able to discuss how Women's New Cinema interrogates stereotypical femininity, I will present an overview of the changes in female representation in the film history of Turkey. The second element is a critical analysis of Yeşim Ustaoğlu's film *Clair Obscur* as the female representation in this film illuminates the differences between the conventional depictions of woman in the cinema of Turkey and the new female image created by Women's New Cinema. I apply a textual approach to analyze the film's plot, characterizations and depiction of female agency. For this analysis, Teresa De Lauretis's understanding of subjectivity as social and historical (1984; 1990a), Anneke Smelik's understanding of subjectivity as a constant becoming (1998), and Asuman Suner's (2006a) concept of resisting female silences are adopted.

The Representation of Women in the Cinema of Turkey

Until the 1950s, Turkish cinema was dominated exclusively by male directors. Women were included as actresses and audiences but excluded from being active in the process of making films as directors. During these early years of Turkish cinema, women were depicted in stereotypical roles as one-dimensional characters in male-dominated narratives (Özgüç 1988, 23) and as characters of low morality who seduce men and have unbridled sexual appetites (Dönmez-Colin 2010, 91). In the 1950s, Yeşilçam films started presenting a different type of female who was characterized as suffering, passive, loyal, and obedient. Agah Özgüç states that this "woman of all sorts of pain" obeys the patriarchal order, is patient and sacrifices or gives up on her own self so as to be rewarded by receiving a proposal for marriage from a male character (Özgüç 1988, 34; Abisel 1994, 136).

Migration from villages in the east to cities in the west in Turkey was one of the consequences of modernization in the country and it deeply affected society during the 1960s. Leaving the traditional village life and confronting the new values of the city created fear amongst society; the fear of "Westoxification," i.e., being tempted by the immorality of the West. This was immediately reflected on the screen in the films of the time. There were two key female archetypes in these films. Some female characters were good and virtuous. Of these characters, Atakav writes:

> The virtuous woman was a good wife to her husband, and obeyed his rules; was a good mother to her children; constantly forgave all slights, insults and betrayals; did not resist even though she felt subordinated; knew how to cry on the inside and never to show her sorrow on the outside (to avoid punishment); and was responsible for keeping the family together and happy. (2013, 48)

The second female archetype was the femme fatale character who disobeys the male order by crossing into the public space. Dressing indecently, dancing and drinking at parties and seducing men were the characteristics of this "bad" urban woman (Dönmez-Colin 2010, 92). The national cinema presented the ideal modernization and urbanization by praising the good women and punishing the bad, spreading the official ideology through filmic representations of women's bodies.

The rise of Yeşilçam continued in the first half of the 1970s; however, the end of the decade witnessed political violence between left and right, a stagnant economy and the arrival of television, which encouraged families to stay in their houses rather than going out to the cinema. Losing its loyal audience, the family, and unable to cope with the rising costs of making films in color, theatres started importing cheap pornographic films (Abisel 1994, 113). These attracted male audiences who enjoyed watching the exploitation of women on screen (Atakav, 2013, 45). The second trend of the era was to produce films problematizing social issues. In these films, the male directors showed female characters "abandon[ing] their desires, wants, needs and wealth," either because they were not strong enough or they did not have the opportunity to make decisions about their own lives (Abisel 1994, 212).

The new values of the neoliberal world met 1980s Turkey. The 1980 military coup transformed citizens into apolitical and lonely individuals while the neoliberal economic policies turned the society into an Americanized "market society" (Bora 2007, 168); in the 1980s, cultural products were reduced to an exchange value and became consumable (Gürbilek 2001, 26–35). The Second Wave feminist movement also arrived in the country and Turkey experienced a strong feminist uprising. The cinema of Turkey reflected these changes with a new genre, "women's films." In an environment where political activism was forbidden and the influence of feminism was felt strongly, directors found a way to produce films that dealt with politics indirectly but were not perceived as political by telling women's stories (Atakav 2013, 3). Contrary to pre-'80s representation, the female characters in these films were not the signifier of man's desire but their own. However, their pursuit of freedom was limited to sexuality. This liberation was not depicted as a feature that profoundly transformed the representation of women.

Neoliberalism, globalization and the 1980s coup triggered deep sociological transformations in 1990s Turkey, and this changed the characteristics of the images reflected on the screen. According to Turkish academic and author Z. Tül Akbal Süalp (2010), the men of this suppressed, weakened, and traumatized society were unemployed, lonely, and apoliticized and were trying to cope with their wounded masculinity and anger. She argues that this state of masculinity is the starting point or even the main issue of the stories of male directors such as Nuri Bilge Ceylan and Zeki Demirkubuz, who produce films within the New Cinema movement. In most narratives, these unemployed, powerless, and angry male characters who suffer from existential and nihilistic problems choose to direct the anger of their bruised pride towards women.

It is worth considering that this state of masculinity was not simply a result of social changes but encouraged by the state. The military state encouraged a culture of manhood that was macho, sociopathic, and sexist to suppress minority groups, such as women, homosexuals, and those from marginalized groups. As Ertuğrul Kürkçü suggests, this conflict created a "low-intensity war" that

> covered every cell of society like a tumor throughout the 90s. Nationalism and racism, whose toxic effects are still as devastating as before; machismo, misogyny, and sexism indispensable in nurturing the human raw material of state violence; hate speech, the most direct tool for suppressing the different and the marginal; xenophobia, which is necessary to block international solidarity, the oppressed and those who struggle; ceaselessly reproduced conservatism, stifling the potential for change inherent in creativity, knowledge and new forms of social relations, seeped into and grew in the 90s. (2014)

It is logical to assume that the "male melodramas" or "arabesque noir" narratives of the male directors of the New Cinema movement are a direct result of this sexist, macho, and misogynist manhood nurtured by the state. The absent, silent female characters of these stories are a consequence of this construction. Women in these melodramas are mere images affirming masculinity. De Lauretis's concept, the "non-being of woman," outlines the absent-subjectivity of the 1990s female image well. De Lauretis describes this concept as

> the paradox of a being that is at once captive and absent in discourse, constantly spoken of but of itself inaudible or inexpressible, displayed as spectacle

> and still unrepresented or unrepresentable, invisible yet constituted as the object and the guarantee of vision; a being whose existence and specificity are simultaneously asserted and denied, negated and controlled. (1990b, 115)

Similarly, in the narratives of the male directors of the New Cinema movement, women are denied, negated, and controlled by the male discourse. In these new wave films, while the viewer can sense his story deeply, the actions of the female character are meaningless and irrational; the narrative reduces her existence. What, then, do we call new in this New Cinema?

From this perspective, nothing seems new; the New Cinema movement is the remasculinization of the cinema of Turkey.

The female directors of Women's New Cinema, however, disrupt this course of events. With its emergence, the contemporary Turkish cinematic scene has witnessed one of the most significant new conceptions: complex female subjectivities. In comparison to the passive, loyal, appropriate, pornographic, or absent female representation of previous decades, the new female representation is depicted in various, multiple experiences.

Analyzing Yeşim Ustaoğlu's film *Clair Obscur* and making parallels with films of other female directors within Women's New Cinema, for the remainder of this chapter I aim to understand the characteristics of this newly emergent female representation that challenges the stereotypical one-dimensionality of female representation in the cinema of Turkey.

Female Character Occupying the Subject Position

Clair Obscur is the sixth fiction film made by Ustaoğlu and it was released in 2016. It tells the intertwined story of two women, Şehnaz and Elmas. Şehnaz is a successful psychiatrist who lives with her husband, Cem, in the city but works in a town. Although everything seems comfortable in her life, she is unhappy in her marriage as her husband, although he looks and acts kind and modern, does not satisfy Şehnaz emotionally or sexually. Elmas is a sixteen-year-old girl who was forced into a marriage to a husband who rapes her almost every night. One morning Elmas is found by the police on her balcony shivering in fear. She is taken to the hospital where Şehnaz works. There we understand that Elmas's husband and his mother were found dead in the house. At the hospital, Elmas, who has experienced a memory lapse, is examined by Şehnaz. Through the therapy sessions, a clear picture of Elmas's life begins to emerge. It was her mother who forced her into marriage and her family took money from her husband upon the marriage. Elmas's anger and fear are dissolved into peace through the catharsis she experiences during the therapy sessions, and with the help of

Elmas, Şehnaz finds the courage to examine her life and face the realities of it. At the end of the film, Şehnaz leaves her husband.

In *Clair Obscur*, Ustaoğlu tells us a new type of story in the cinema of Turkey because it has a women-centered narrative. Ustaoğlu chooses to tell the stories of women who are not punished for their decisions or actions, which is an unusual form of storytelling in the cinema of Turkey, which has historically prioritized male stories, told in films directed by men. Although I chose *Clair Obscur* to analyze here as it provides me with various discussion points in relation to which my argument unfolds, Ustaoğlu's filmography includes many more female stories. In *Waiting for the Clouds*, she tells the story of Ayşe/Eleni who lost her Greek identity during the forced immigration from Turkey to Greece; in her documentary, *Sırtlarındaki Hayat/Life on Their Shoulders* (2004), she depicts the lives of Black Sea peasant women; in *Pandora's Box*, she tells us the story of a mother with Alzheimer's; and in *Araf/Somewhere in Between* (2012), she narrates the life of a young working-class woman, Zehra. With the rise of women's cinema, Turkey has more female stories with female protagonists. Mina from *Present Tense*, Nesrin and Hatun from *Dust Cloth*, Hasret from *Inflame*, Zühre from *Saklı Yüzler/Hidden Faces* (İpekçi, 2007), Nesrin from *Motherland*, Sevda and Zuhal from *What Remains*, the peasant women from *The Play* and *Queen Lear* are a few examples of the new female faces of the screen.

Ustaoğlu, like many other contemporary female directors of Women's New Cinema, revises the female image in *Clair Obscur* by making women the narrative agents of their own lives; their decisions control the course of the narrative. Elmas (Figure 2.1) tells us "her" story, where she alters her tragic "fate" and builds her own life with the help of Şehnaz. Elmas chooses to live her own life instead of the life chosen for her by her family and enforced by her husband.

Figure 2.1 Elmas, the female protagonist of *Clair Obscur*.

At the end of the film, she is depicted as hopeful; she is not punished because of her choice or because she murdered her raping husband and his torturing mother. Male justice does not prevail. Within the same story, Şehnaz is depicted as a woman who owns her desire and acts on it. Unlike traditional narratives in which female characters with sexual desire are fated to have an unhappy ending, where they may even end up dying, Şehnaz finds the courage to be the subject of her own life. She chooses to find satisfaction with a different partner and decides not to continue with her unsatisfying marriage. The last scene, in which she half laughs and half cries, reveals how freedom feels.

Situating the female figure as the subject of the narrative allows us to focus on the close relationship between the subject and knowledge production, the latter holding the power to build individuals. The policies on women enforced by the Turkish state (either secular or neoliberal Islamist) and the state's ideological apparatus,[3] such as popular culture (commercials, TV series, newspapers and magazines), high culture (art cinema), moral discourses, family traditions, and legal discourses, are all arranged to control the female body. For decades, part of this apparatus, male-dominated cinematic narratives, have not depicted women as characters owning a story but instead showed clichéd images of femininity in support of hegemonic ideology. Using the ideas of Budd Boetticher, Laura Mulvey points out the "alien presence" of female characters in the narrative:

> What counts is what the heroine provokes, or rather what she represents. She is the one, or rather the love or fear she inspires in the hero, or else the concern he feels for her, who makes him act the way he does. In herself the woman has not the slightest importance. (1999, 63)

For decades in the cinema of Turkey female characters were simply appendices to male stories; in themselves, they were of no value. What the female directors within Women's New Cinema have done is reconstruct the female image as the agent of her own life. In this sense, emerging female directors produce alternative representations of women's lives in the contemporary cinema of Turkey through their depictions of complex female characters.

In a sociopolitical atmosphere in which women are denied any plurality in identity, Women's New Cinema depicts female characters that are in constant transformation rather than fixed in one identity. This new characterization fits with Smelik's understanding of subjectivity as a "process of continuous becoming rather than as a state of being" (1998, 3). Smelik evaluates female subjectivity not as fixed but in constant transformation, which gives women the power to become something else than what they are socially programmed to be (1998, 3). However, her becoming something else than what she is expected to be does not mean that Women's New Cinema creates only positive female images. Thinking through Stuart Hall's theory on representation, which argues that "revers[ing] the stereotype is not necessarily to overturn or subvert it" ([1997] 2017, 353–5), I evaluate these new female images not as anti-clichés (which are also clichés) that function in opposition to the clichéd images produced by male-dominated narratives nor as positive female images, as that homogenizes all "others" who are not white, male, and heterosexual and which continues the creation of binaries. In this sense, Women's New Cinema is about challenging stereotypes by creating female characters who have more complex characterization than women from earlier Turkish films. In this regard, Women's New Cinema calls into question the official discourse by inviting the audience to remember that it is possible to become someone else and not just adjusting one's self to be what is socially expected.

Besides challenging stereotypes with more complex characterization, Women's New Cinema also interrogates stereotypical femininity by depicting female characters who are "historically and socially situated" (De Lauretis 1990a, 17). Ustaoğlu constructs women as a "historical and social subject," which means the female image reflects the current struggles of the feminist agenda in Turkey such as violence, gendercide (female genocide), early-age marriages and family oppression. In *Merry-Go-Round*, İlksen Başarır addresses pedophilia; in *The Play*, Pelin Esmer addresses violence against women; while family oppression is addressed by Deniz Akçay in *Nobody's Home*, Senem Tüzen in *Motherland*, and Emine Emel Balcı in *Until I Lose My Breath*. These films represent the female subject in ways that engage with the current and the real issues of feminist circles in Turkey.

While reflecting the ongoing sociopolitical situation of women from Turkey, these directors open space for the female protagonists to confront their ongoing situation. Luce Irigaray states that the act of confrontation within women's artwork is an individual and social attempt at purification. To her, showing the courage to express individual and social pains publicly has a therapeutic effect that relieves the pain of the body and allows it to move to another time (2006, 113, 114). Women's New Cinema makes the confronting female characters visible in public space and gives us a chance to reflect upon gender issues while watching these courageous female characters face their ongoing situations which echo women's common lived experience in Turkey. However, these films contain moments where the gaze of the female protagonists is turned towards the viewer (Figure 2.2), and it is as if the female directors are confronting the viewer directly. These moments challenge the viewer to think critically about their lives. This new way of representing women is not about being correct or incorrect but about deconstructing the usual codes, creating new ways of

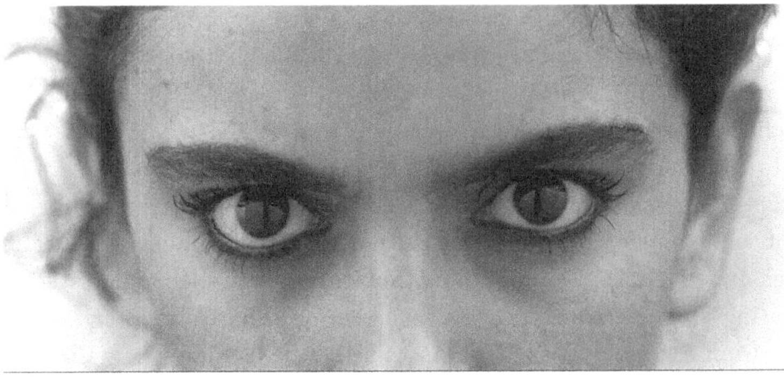

Figure 2.2 A still from *Present Tense* where the audience confronts the female protagonist.

seeing and leaving room for gender critique. As Irigaray and De Lauretis suggest, confrontation within women's artwork is a social attempt at representing the ongoing realities of life on a larger scale and a suggestion to live *otherwise*.

These confronting female subjects reach and reveal the situations of their lives in two ways: through speaking and through resisting within their silence. A good example of the speaking subject is Elmas from *Clair Obscur*. Staying at the hospital under the supervision of Şehnaz, Elmas gets regular therapy sessions that slowly improve her memory. During the therapy sessions, Şehnaz uses a psychodrama technique where Elmas role-reverses; that is, performs both her own persona and her mother's. The role-reversal turns into a confrontation when her mother does not oppose her getting married. Then Elmas makes the speech she expects from her mother. This role-play leads to catharsis and she is freed from the burden of her heavy past. In adopting Irigaray's approach, Elmas's confrontation can be seen as both individual and social. She shows the courage to speak her individual pains publicly, which helps her to heal. Watching her confronting her family has a therapeutic effect that allows the viewers to relieve the pain they suffered through her experience. The length of the therapy session and the gaps Ustaoğlu leaves in the narrative position the viewers to reflect on their own lives and think critically about gender issues. Pelin Esmer's *The Play*, which is addressed in a more detailed way in Chapter 5, offers another powerful example worth mentioning briefly here. The documentary shows the preparation of a theatre play in which the village women act their daily experiences including the difficulties of being a woman, being a mother, and facing family oppression and physical violence. Voicing their experiences stops them from being perceived as victims but instead positions them as the owners of their lives. They are aware that it is their families and their village that will watch this play and that it has the potential to reach a global audience through the production of the documentary. Courageously confronting the situations of their "private" lives in these public spaces frees them from the confining social codes. They transform; they become something other than what they are socially expected to be.

Female silence, however, is a complex issue. Turkish culture establishes silence as a virtue belonging to women. But Ruken Öztürk and Nilgün Tutal remind us that as we remained silent, we remained outside the historical order. When we are included in historicity by using our voice, we have remained foreign due to the masculine language; our words are split/cut off (Öztürk and Tutal 2001, 108, 110). The same order is valid for the cinematic realm, where the image of the woman replaces her voice. In classical narrative, she is exiled not only from the visuality in the active/subject position but also from the field of discourse. The authority of sight and sound is male (2001, 108, 110), as in the case of the male-dominated narratives of the New Cinema Movement where women are victimized and passivized through being made silent. Female directors are also kept silent for decades by not having their work produced, distributed or selected for screening. But women's cinema transforms the meaning of silence. Through silence, woman can resist male oppression. Asuman Suner explains "resisting female silences" by adapting the concept of French film theorist Michel Chion:

> Michel Chion says that another element that functions similarly to the figure of the "silent" in the cinema is the "screaming point." According to Chion, who points out the gender-based difference between the words "shout" and "scream" in English, a man's cry is always aimed at a desire for power, to draw the boundaries of his own space, to dominate within it, while a woman's cry begins where boundaries, words and meanings end. The scream, which creates a kind of black hole in the story world of the film, points beyond the symbolic order, to the place where meaning ends. (2006a, 311–12)

That is how some silences become the screaming points in Women's New Cinema; they start where meaning, words, and language end. It is in this sense they are the indicators of resistance. Ustaoğlu's film *Waiting for the Clouds* sets a good example for resisting female silences. Upon being adopted by a Muslim-Turkish family during forced immigration from Turkey to Greece, the female protagonist of the film, Eleni, becomes Ayşe. She has to leave her Greek identity; she starts speaking Turkish and acts Turkish. Upon losing the last member of her Turkish family, she stops speaking. Specifically, she stops speaking Turkish, the code of a structure that oppressed her Greek identity and led to her losing her own identity. With her silence, she does not simply refuse to talk but refuses the dominant culture; she stops having to be Turkish. After her silent period, the first words coming out of her mouth are in Greek; her silence helps her transform and she comes back as Eleni. In this way, Ustaoğlu uses silence as a language where Eleni resists the male-dominated systems and creates a space where she can become herself rather than being what society forced her to be.

White, heterosexual, male-dominated systems not only depict women in certain ways but also determine the visual norms. That is why "it would be appropriate to move the masculine gaze in Turkey's representation and image repertoire towards a cultural curtain that works together with other inequalities" (U. T. Arslan 2022b). Using the term "curtain of Turkishness," Arslan draws attention to the "skills and oppressive power of this curtain in producing dominant, normative selves that determine who will be seen and how" (2022b). Until the beginning of the 2000s, the female representation constructed by the female and male directors of both popular and art cinema was in alignment with the visual norms of the same curtain (Kurdish cinema is an exception to this). Cinema was representing either white, Turkish, urban, educated, and middle-class women or white, Turkish, rural, and traditional women. However, Women's New Cinema, by paving ways to rethink and question what life and politics mean in terms of being working-class, Greek/Kurdish/Armenian and Muslim[4] deconstructs the one-dimensionality of representation. Contrary to the traditional depiction of women (either as someone's mother or someone's wife), contemporary female directors employ diverse female identities and enable the audience to see together with the "other." In this sense, Women's New Cinema "derives its ethical power from the openness to otherness and heterogeneity of both women and each individual woman" (U. T. Arslan 2022c).

These realistic representations do not align with the expectations of the main audience segment who enjoys watching the white, modern but traditional, heterosexual or genderless mothers and wives in comedy films. As it contradicts the expectations within Turkey, it contradicts the expectations of the West that desires to see Eastern women as victims of religion, patriarchy, tradition, and poverty. Resisting the construction of a unique national identity and of universalizing womanhood, these female representations bring "a simultaneous critique both of Third-Worldist anti-colonial nationalism and of First World Eurocentric feminism" (Shohat 2003, 52), bringing accented feminist theories[5] into discussion. *Waiting for the Clouds* (2003), for instance, drawing the oppression of the Turkish structure over a story of a Greek woman, is not designed to appeal to the Westerncentric desire that would see Ayşe/Eleni as the victim of the Turkish patriarchal order.[6] Ustaoğlu refuses to testify to this presumed condition; setting a sample reflecting the heterogeneities of the struggles of Eastern women, she deconstructs the imagery of a composite singular third world womanhood.

Constructing Ayşe/Eleni's gender identity together with her race, she brings a criticism towards the Turkish nationalism and the ideology of contemporary neo-colonialism as well. *Qiblenameya Deya Min/My Mother's Compass* (Kamer, 2013) sets another good example with its subversive story. The film tells the story of a Kurdish mother who visits her son in exile in Norway. Unlike the major narratives telling the "exotic" stories of Western women in East, in *My Mother's Compass* the audience sees the journey of a Middle Eastern woman to Europe. Instead of reproducing stereotyped representations of Middle Eastern women who enjoy the freedoms offered by West, transform and fit the modern world immediately, Behiye (the protagonist) does not enjoy Norway and criticizes its "unusual" way of living life. In this sense, Women's New Cinema not only deconstructs the national, institutional identity that is "people from Turkey are Turks," but also focuses on gender in relation to race and class. It "fails" to assimilate and meet the expectations of universalizing Western feminism.

The directors of Women's New Cinema also reject the assigned roles of women by refusing to present female characters as conflicting parties. For decades, female identity in cinema in Turkey functioned as a tool to construct conflict in cinematic narratives. Functioning as a tool promoting the state's ideology, conventional cinema created binaries such as traditional woman versus modern woman—it dictated the ideal womanhood. In the same way, it created a conflicting point in the dichotomy of the good woman who is a "traditionally modern" mother protecting her family, and the bad, urban woman who seduces men with her Westernized pleasures. In these narratives, the female character was either a plump brunette with Middle Eastern features, charming the local audience (Büker 2002, 15), or she was a blonde, serving the narrative as the femme fatale. Although the female characters of *Clair Obscur* have the stereotyped features—for example, modern/traditional, educated/uneducated, rural/urban, housewife/middle-class—which make them available for binaries, Ustaoğlu chooses to construct the relationship between Elmas and Şehnaz as one of solidarity. Instead of emphasizing their differences in a narrative where Şehnaz, a member of elite class, helps the poor, uneducated Elmas, Ustaoğlu depicts their differences as a natural consequence of being a social subject and underlines the similarities of both women struggling to be the subjects of their lives against the oppression of male-dominated culture. Belmin Söylemez's *Present Tense* also has a special perspective in terms of the relationships between women. "Instead of knowing each other and oneself completely and merging, it allows us to imagine relationality and transformation by opening up to each other" (U. T. Arslan 2022c). In *Dust Cloth*, there is another kind of solidarity between the characters Nesrin, who leaves the life she can no longer endure, and Hatun, who becomes the chosen family of Nesrin's daughter after Nesrin leaves.

In *Waiting for the Clouds*, Ustaoğlu shows solidarity between the village women, especially Feride, who supports Ayşe/Eleni's transformation and her finding of her true self.

The contemporary female directors of Women's New Cinema not only create different conflict points within their stories but also assign different characteristics to the stereotyped roles. For example, in *Dust Cloth*, *Zephyr*, *Nobody's Home*, and *Motherland*, the sacred mother archetype is destroyed. Neither Ahu Öztürk, the director of *Dust Cloth*, nor Belma Baş, the director of *Zephyr*, prefers to demonize the mother character because she chooses to leave her child behind to be able to live her own life. In *Nobody's Home* and *Motherland*, the directors construct a critical statement about traditional motherhood by reflecting the destructive power of traditional values. On the other hand, Emine Emel Balcı in *Until I Lose My Breath* creates a daughter character, Serap, but she constructs her as an anti-heroine. Ripping Serap from the traditional attributes of being a daughter, such as respecting the father, obeying his rules etc., the director makes the audience, who are not accustomed to anti-heroines, witness the story of a young woman, feel the dilemmas of Serap. In *What Remains*, Çiğdem Vitrinel seems to create a conflict between a mother/wife, Sevda, and a femme fatale, Zuhal; however, these characters are reflected from an entirely different point of view. It is not Cezmi, the husband of Sevda and the lover of Zuhal who determines the flow of events, it is rather the choices of the female characters that shape the storyline. In this story, the innocent one is not the mother/wife who is betrayed by her husband, and it is not the femme fatale that is the immoral woman. Sevda is a conformist woman who murders Zuhal to protect her status. Zuhal, on the other hand, is a working-class, single mother. She is in a relationship with Sevda's husband, and the director depicts her as a moral, righteous character in this story. The audience identifies with Zuhal which is an unusual narrative for the cinema of Turkey. Contemporary female directors construct their female characters away from the cliché codes of womanhood—they create neither mothers nor prostitutes, but provide us with alternative womanhood. They construct a critical statement towards the norms and codes of society.

Deconstructing Male Image

While reconstructing the female image, Women's New Cinema deconstructs the male image and the current codes of masculinity. It attempts to create the imagery of a new masculinity. In *Journey to the Sun*, *Fakat Müzeyyen Bu Derin Bir Tutku* (Vitrinel, 2014), *Lifelong*, *What Remains*, and *Peri Tozu* (Alyamaç, 2008), the male characters go through a transformation and gain post-masculinist features. Despite having difficult experiences, they are depicted as gentle, caring, and tolerant. They recognize and experience their emotions. This new masculinity threatens the patriarchal culture and the male-dominated cinema nurtured by this culture.

Contemporary female directors deconstruct the male image also by subverting the conventional flow of the narrative. Despite having box office success as romances, *Bir Avuç Deniz/A Handful of Sea* (Yılmaz, 2011) and *Başka Dilde Aşk/ Love in Another Language* (Başarır, 2009) still present their non-conventional feminist ideas by changing the gaze, disrupting the order between the seen and the seer. The female protagonists of these films, Deniz and Zeynep, often use their cameras to take pictures of the male protagonists, Mert and Onur. Their being behind the viewfinder places the male characters in the object position. In these films, women are not exhibited to please the male gaze, but they are the active subjects bearing the gaze. This turns men into objects being looked at. The act of being looked at makes men unsettled while spoiling their pleasure as seers. Disrupting the visual order and opening a space for new masculinity to thrive, these films are feminist interventions, and their reaching box office success as romantic films does not make them any less women's films. In this sense, I would like to challenge the approach of feminist film studies posing the popular/ commercially successful women's films as an antidote to art/avant-garde cinema. I prefer evaluating these films as a part of Women's New Cinema because women's films can position the experience of women in the center of the narration by adapting either alternative stylistic features or conventional ones but using the latter to transfer their non-conventional feminist ideas. This approach might enable us to define feminist cinema free from rigid, binary structures (e.g., alternative vs mainstream, avant-garde vs classical narrative cinema).

Another often repeated and striking feature of the male representation constructed within Women's New Cinema is their lack of individuality. Similar to Deleuze's concept of "any space whatsoever," that is a whatever space such as a metro stop, or an airport terminal which is not even a space but a point of transit people pass through (see Bell 1997), I name this male character as any-man-whomsoever. An any-man-whomsoever is the man who is an anybody. We do not know where he comes from, or his job; we often do not even know his name. In *Clair Obscur*, for instance, we do not meet Elmas's husband; we do not know his name, his likes and dislikes, his daily routine, or his job. Similarly, in *Merry-Go-Round*, the time period, the town, and the place where the male character works are all ambiguous. By constructing male characters who are not individuals, the directors can construct a critical statement about the masculinist society. Surprisingly, the male characters of these films are murdered by their wives, but what is punished here is not the male character but the entire patriarchal culture that oppresses women.

Conclusion: Finally, the Cinema of Turkey Has Female Stories

Yesterday at a conference, I listened to the Aboriginal (Wiradjuri) transgender scholar Sandy O'Sullivan talking about the rarity of queer Indigenous representation on Australian TV (O'Sullivan 2023). This information reminded me of the story of Claudia, who is the narrator of *The Bluest Eye*, the first novel written by Toni Morrison. One Christmas, Claudia receives a "blue-eyed, yellow haired, pink-skinned doll" for which she feels no affection; she says, "I could not love it but I could examine it to see what it was that all the world said was loveable" (Morrison 1998, 21). According to Morrison, the doll is the representation of the "Master Narrative:"

> whatever ideological script that is being imposed by the people in authority on everybody else: The Master Fiction . . . history. It has a certain point of view. So when those little girls see that the most prized gift they can receive at Christmas time is this little white doll, that's the Master Narrative speaking: this is beautiful, this is lovely, and you're not it, so what are you going to do about it? (Morrison quoted in Moyers 1990)

Master Narrative tells the stories of blue-eyed, yellow haired, pink-skinned dolls, not the stories of Blacks, queers, and the unwanted others. What are we going to do about it? I find the answer in Audre Lorde; she reminds us that if we do not define ourselves for ourselves, we can be crunched into other people's fantasies for us (Master Narrative) and eaten alive ([1984] 2007, 137). This is exactly why Women's New Cinema attempts to tell other stories; it tells our stories back to us creatively.

For many decades, the male-dominated cinema of Turkey, or the Master Cinema as I can call it, has spread official ideology through women's bodies and told its female audiences what ideal womanhood looks like. However, the contemporary female directors of Women's New Cinema deconstruct this stereotyped womanhood and reconstruct the female image within women-centered narratives; that is, women in these stories are the narrative agents of their own lives. Assigning their subjectivity, the female directors present the female image not as an object or a fetish but as a character whose experiences contribute the meaning to the film. These new films construct the feminist subject as the producer of meaning, the narratives are designed to reveal the story from the female point of view. The conflict points are no longer built between good and bad woman, urban and traditional woman, the directors tell us stories strengthened by female solidarity. Women's New Cinema shows us women stand up and rise up together. It deconstructs the normative roles of motherhood and womanhood and provides us with new ways of being a woman, for instance as an anti-heroine. This signs a radical transformation from the cinema of fathers and sons into a cinema where we watch women speaking out, singing, and seeking the remedy within themselves, among themselves.

Contemporary female directors construct the female image as a "historical and social subject" that reflects the current struggles of a feminist agenda in Turkey; that is, the individual troubles of any female character present a micro sample of "being a woman" in Turkey. Depicting diverse female identities—for example, working-class woman, Greek or Kurdish woman, non-Muslim woman, woman with different sexual orientation or sexual identity—Women's New Cinema deconstructs the one-dimensionality of representation. These realistic representations do not align with the expectations of the main audience that enjoys watching the white, traditional, and genderless mothers and wives. As they contradict the expectations within Turkey, they contradict the expectations of the West which desires to see Eastern women as victims of religion, patriarchy, tradition, and poverty. These representations reveal multiple and complex existences of Eastern women spoiling the Eurocentric universalizing of womanhood that assumes an already formed, coherent group with identical needs, desires, and objections.

While reconstructing the female image, Women's New Cinema deconstructs the male image and the current codes of masculinity; it attempts to create the imagery of a new masculinity. The new male image built by the contemporary female directors is gentle, understanding, tolerant, and recognizes his emotions. Another characteristic of this new male image is its being an any-man-whomsoever, that is he is an anybody. In these narratives, the criticism is not aimed at that individual man within the storyline but towards the masculinist society; that might be why the directors erase the man's individuality, identity.

The contemporary female directors of Women's New Cinema work on gender and deliberately oppose the prevalent gender and sexual definitions. With their new female imagery that is in constant transformation, constant becoming, they gain women the power to become something else than what they are socially programmed to be. Depicting the male character at peace with his emotions, they deconstruct the masculinity and subvert the macho codes of the social order. With its unusual characters (unusual in the sense that we are not used to watching such characters), Women's New Cinema reminds us of the wide range of possibilities in life.

Notes

1. Arabesque noir is one of the manifestations of the renewed effect of the film noir style in Turkish cinema. It consists of male melodramas in which the genre of film noir is an inevitable backdrop to the sensitivities of the bored male protagonists, mostly with a mystical existentialism (Süalp 2009, 4).

2. Vasfiye is the female protagonist of the film *Adı Vasfiye/Her Name is Vasfiye* (Yılmaz, 1985). In the film, the story of Vasfiye is told by different men and her voice is not heard until the end of the movie. Suner states that the character of Vasfiye has become a trend in New Cinema. She argues that the stories of the new wave films are based on the "absence of women" and the narrative unfolds through their silence.
3. Ideological state apparatus is a concept developed by Louis Althusser using Marxist state theory. The state uses apparatuses such as religion, family, education, law, politics, trade unions, communication, and culture in order to spread its official ideologies without force (2006, 63–4).
4. Chapter 3 is dedicated to this diversity.
5. Accented feminism, a term I coined, is discussed in a detailed way in Chapter 3.
6. See Asuman Suner's essay "Cinema without Frontiers: Transnational Women's Filmmaking in Iran and Turkey" (2007, 53–70) that comparatively analyzes *Waiting for the Clouds* (2003) and *Blackboards* (Makhmalbaf, 2000).

Chapter 3

Her Resistance is Many: The Accented Filmmaking Practice in Women's New Cinema[1]

I would like to start this chapter by retelling a story told by Hrant Dink, who was a Turkish-Armenian intellectual, journalist, and activist.

> An uncle[2] from a district of Sivas [a city in central Turkey] called me. He said:
>
> — Son, we searched and found you. There is an old woman here, obviously, she belongs to your community. She has passed away. If you find a relative of her, they can come and pick her up, or we will perform our prayers here and bury her.
> — Okay, uncle, I'll call you.
>
> A woman named Ms. Beatris at the age of 70 went there from France. I searched and found who she was within 10 minutes. We know each other because we are very few. I went to a store, gave her name, and asked:
>
> — Do you know her?
>
> A woman turned and said:
>
> — She is my mother.
> — Where is your mother?
> — Brother, she lives in France.
> — Does she often come here?
> — She comes to Turkey three or four times a year but rarely visits Istanbul. She goes to Kalkar village, the village we abandoned.
>
> I told her about the phone call I received. She went to Kalkar. She called me the next day. She found her mother and identified her. I said:
>
> — Will you bring the body?
> — I'll bring it, but there is an uncle here.

And she started to cry.

— Give the phone to the uncle . . . Uncle, why are you making her cry?
— Son, I didn't say anything. I told her that it was her mother but if she asked me, she should let her stay and be buried here. The water found its crack . . .

I was shattered. I was shattered with this saying of the Anatolian people. I was shattered due to this perception. Yes, "the water found its crack." It is true, Armenians do have their eyes on this country [Turkey]. We have an eye on this land. Let me repeat to you what I wrote to the newspaper then. At that time, Mr. President Demirel said:

— We won't even give three pebbles [from this land] to the Armenians.

I wrote Beatris' story. And I said:

— Yes, we Armenians have our eyes on these lands. Because our roots are here. But don't worry. We have an eye on it, not to come and cease it but to reach its base . . . (H. Dink 2005)

Hrant Dink dedicated his life to advancing peace, cultural dialogue and empathy between Turkish and Armenian communities but he was assassinated in front of Agos, his newspaper's office in Istanbul, in 2007. I wanted to start this chapter with a story told by a Turkish-Armenian peacemaker who was assassinated in his home country.[3] The stories of Beatris and Hrant can open a window from which we can see the entire political, social, and historical processes experienced by the "minorities" living in Turkey. Within these stories, we can also witness the resilience and resistance of these vulnerable groups.

In this chapter, I will focus on the "accented" filmmaking model in Women's New Cinema which I read as a resistance technique practiced by "minority" women filmmakers. Focusing particularly on *I Flew You Stayed* (2012) made by the Kurdish female director Mizgin Müjde Arslan, I aim to provide a space for the experiences of the "other" women who live under the hegemony of Turkish structure. For this, I will apply the theory of diasporic film theorized as "accented cinema" by Hamid Naficy (2001, 8). Accented cinema describes the exilic state of filmmakers who either move from the third world countries to the West or live in the diaspora (2001, 8).[4] For Naficy (2001, 4), cinema is not accented because the filmmaker speaks with an accent, it is rather her deterritorialization and the artisanal mode of production that make her cinema accented. Asuman Suner

(2006b), on the other hand, claims that a film that shares the "cinematic styles and thematic preoccupations associated with exilic/diasporic films" can be categorized as accented even though it belongs to a national cinema with a director living in their home country. Her definition of accented cinema includes national films dealing with the situation of minority groups living under dominant cultures, a theme shared by accented films. She underlines the "exilic state" of these groups within their "own homeland, community, and language" (Suner 2010, 73) and suggests to employ Naficy's model to evaluate the "minority" protagonists or directors born or living in Turkey. Her definition of accented cinema includes national films dealing with the situation of minority groups living under the hegemony of dominant cultures.

Asuman Suner (2007) furthers Naficy's model by involving transnational feminist filmmaking practices within accented film discussions. As Naficy's model lacks the gender dimension in its imagery of nation, identity, and belonging, I will discuss Naficy's model in a broader context by adapting Suner's understanding and adding the gender dimension into my perspective. For this purpose, I will use the principles of "accented feminism," a term I will develop in this paper and further Suner's perspective. Analyzing these components helps me to draw the concept of "accented feminist cinema," intervene with the whiteness of feminist film theory, and reveal the accented characteristic of Women's New Cinema. Evaluating accented feminist filmmaking practice as a resistance technique against the violence of the official discourse, I aim to reveal how Women's New Cinema offers possibilities of reading the pasts and imagining the futures in an alternative way.

The Principles of Accented Cinema

Accented Director and Accented Characters

Mizgin Müjde Arslan is an accented female director not because of her exilic status—she produced the majority of her filmography while living in Turkey—but because she was culturally exilic: she was living as a "minority" under the hegemony of the Turkish state and the domination of Turkish culture. Naficy (2001, 8) requires the director's deterritorialization as a corporeal experience in constructing his theory of accented cinema. Here, he refers both to "a cinema *of* exile and a cinema *in* exile" (2001, 8; original emphasis). Suner (2010, 73), on the other hand, extends the limits of his theory by suggesting that a director can experience an exilic state within her own homeland, and thus carries the culturally exilic state into the discussions of accented cinema. In alignment with Suner's approach, I count Mizgin Müjde Arslan as an accented director; she is a

Kurdish director who produced many films under the conditions of hegemonic Turkish structure.

I Flew You Stayed, released in 2012, is Arslan's third documentary. It is a self-reflexive and ethnographic film about Arslan's search for her father.[5] The autobiographical nature of the documentary is the conscious choice of the director; she states she wants to tell personal stories because when she was a child, it was her motivation to survive and tell her story to the world. That is why, instead of narrating "their" stories, she prefers to tell stories that include herself from her personal perspective (Fontini 2024b, 5). This autobiographical self-reflexivity, which is a common motif in accented cinema (Naficy 2001, 276–7), strengthens Arslan's authorial statement as a female director and doubles her effect as a person who performs not only her directorial personality but also as the subject of the film.

In addition to the exilic state of the director, the exilic state of the characters and the audience can make a film accented (Naficy 2001, 23) and there are several such instances in Women's New Cinema. For example Berke Baş's *Hush!* narrates the events of 1915 over the silenced story of the director's grandmother; Nezahat Gündoğan's *Two Locks of Hair: The Lost Girls of Dersim* and *Unburied in The Past—The Missing Girls of The Dersim* feature the Kurdish-Alevi massacre of 1937, telling the story of the little girls distributed to military families. Melisa Önel's *Me and Nuri Bala* tells the personal story of Esmeray, a Kurdish transsexual activist and artist, Yeşim Ustaoğlu's *Waiting for the Clouds* examines the forced migration of Greek families from Turkey during World War II through the character of Ayşe/Eleni, who hides her identity for decades after being adopted by a Turkish family. Hatice Kamer's *My Mother's Compass* (2013) narrates the journey of a Kurdish mother who visits her son who lives in exile in Norway, and *Jinen Dengbej/Women Dengbeji* (Atölyemor Kolektifi, 2007) tells the stories of Kurdish women who preserve their culture through singing the history and experience of Kurdish society despite the objections of their families and community. These films show the characteristics of accented cinema with their Kurdish, Armenian, and Greek characters living under the hegemonic Turkish structure and their audience living in exile.

Journeys and Deterritorialization

Another major theme in accented cinema is journeying. Naficy determines three types of journey modalities in accented films (2001, 223, 290): (1) "outward journeys of escape" or "search for a home" journeys emphasize the reasons causing the exile; (2) "home seeking" journeys underline "lostness," "wandering," "displacement," and "homelessness"; and (3) "home founding" journeys are about "the return," "the desire to return," and "the impossibility to return." These modes of journey are accompanied by three types of cinematic chronotopes, which are "specific temporal and spatial settings in which stories unfold" (2001, 152): (1) "open chronotopes" indicate "boundlessness and timelessness" while symbolizing the idealized homeland; (2) "closed chronotopes" indicate claustrophobia and temporality symbolizing life in exile; and (3) "thirdspace chronotopes" are border spaces such as hotels, cars, buses, and tunnels (2001, 153).

The narrative of *I Flew You Stayed* includes all three types of journeys and chronotopes described in Naficy's model. An analysis of the story of this documentary highlights the use of the journey modalities. The film opens with a conversation Arslan has with her mother about why she has decided to make a journey to discover the story of her father, Ahmet, who was killed in the Mahmur camp in Iraq. In the next scene, Arslan is in a car beginning her journey. She first goes to her village and visits her grandparents. Here she discovers many photographs and letters written by Ahmet, hears his voice played from a cassette, and listens to the childhood memories of her grandmother. These are mostly sad memories, such as the political reasons forcing her family to move from their homeland of Turkey to Iraq and the family's decision to take their son with them but leave Arslan behind in Turkey to be raised by her grandparents. We see Arslan talking to her father's best friend and visiting her aunt and uncle to learn more about the reasons why her father left and more details about his personality. She takes the bus to Cizre, where she meets several people who drive her and the camerawoman, Özay Şahin, to Erbil. They stay in a house with people who will take them to the grave of Ahmet. There she learns about her father's kind nature, listens to stories of how he became the father of many orphan children in the immigration camp and how he was killed while defending the safety of the camp. The next day, Arslan learns that they are not allowed to go to the region where her father's grave might be because they carry Turkish passports and are filming their journey. Though Arslan cannot find her father's grave, she hears many memories related to him. At the end of the film, she confronts her mother, who took her son but left her behind while joining her husband in Syria. Arslan asks her one of the biggest questions of her life: "Why did you leave me behind?" (Fontini 2024b, 2).

Arslan's journey starts from her grandparent's village. In these scenes, we see nature, a vast landscape, giving us a sense of boundlessness and timelessness. It is Arslan's idealized homeland depicted in an open chronotope configuration. In one particular close-up scene, we see her gazing upon the vast landscape of mountains. In accented films, mountains as well as monuments and ruins are significant presences, especially for Kurdish, Palestinian, and

Armenian nations. They are the indicators of the entire idea of nation and the nation's controversial status. Such natural and cultural aspects are "collective chronotopes" that do not separate geographies or people but function as a bridge constructing the idea of a nation (Naficy 2001, 160). However, in Arslan's case, rather than evoking a national image, the mountain is the place where she lost her father. In this sense, the collective chronotope turns into a closed chronotope which reminds Arslan of her father's forced exile and her past without a father. In the following scene, we watch Arslan's "search for a home." She asks her grandmother personal questions like who she is, where she comes from, and questions about her past, shadowing her present and her family's exile. This does not imply a territorial journey, but instead a psychological one—an inward journey, a search for home, for an identity. In this sense, the film is a process of becoming. In the next part of the narrative, Arslan takes a "home-seeking" journey to find out about her father. Arslan had no idea about the places that they were travelling to. She and the camerawoman were filled with fear that something terrible would happen when they crossed the border (Fontini 2024b, 6). They travelled by car, by bus, and through tunnels. They passed through many places and by many people until they crossed the "uncanny" border. During this journey, we see a contrasting dialectic between the claustrophobic atmosphere inside the vehicles and the openness offered by nature outside of the vehicles. All of these are the symbols of displacement, temporality, and the lostness belonging to the thirdspace chronotope configuration. In the end, she cannot find her father's grave and returns to her mother's house.

The more deeply we analyze the stylistic features of Arslan's documentary, the better we see how her choices are shaped by limitations. The need to arrange the camera according to the spatial aspects allows us to observe two cinematic forms in alignment with spatial chronotopes: "open and closed stylistic forms" (Naficy 2001, 153). In the open configuration scheme, we see the characters outside in bright daylight and broad space in which they and the camera can move freely. In these scenes the camera is either static, taking long shots situating characters in open spatial forms, or mobile, shaking while following the characters' movements. Closed spatial forms such as Arslan's and her relatives' houses consist of interior settings, allowing tight compositions with static framing because of the restricted interior area (Figure 3.2). While the mood of closed cinematic form is restriction, gloominess and claustrophobia, it simultaneously represents wandering, seeking, memory, nostalgia, and hope in open cinematic form (Figure 3.1).

Arslan practices a similar approach in her other films. Her first documentary, *Kirasê Mirinê Hewîtî/A Fatal Dress: Polygamy* (2009), focuses on the problem of the tradition of polygamy in the Eastern/Kurdish regions of Turkey. In this film,

Figure 3.1 Open-form cinematic style. The scene is from *I Flew You Stayed.*

Figure 3.2 Closed-form cinematic style. The scene is from *I Flew You Stayed.*

neither the director nor the Kurdish women she interviews have actual journeys. Their journeys take place rather on a psychological level. With each memory they unfold, they have a journey towards their inner selves, their personal lives. As it is the patriarchal norms of the society that cause their exile (from their freedom/independency), they seek their original home, their original selves. In this sense, the psychological journeys they take are "home seeking" journeys underlining their displaced position and homelessness. The director uses "closed chronotopes" to depict this displaced/misplaced position. She interviews the women mostly in their homes where they are stuck, evoking a spaceless and claustrophobic atmosphere (Figure 3.3).

Another strong characteristic of accented cinema is the "deterritorialised style, which is driven by its own limitations, that is, by its smallness, imperfection, amateurishness, and lack of cinematic gloss . . . and narrative intensiveness" (Naficy 2001, 4, 45). Both the content and the style of *I Flew You Stayed* show signs of the accented mode of production. Starting from her own family, Arslan argues the politics of the everyday within her films in which the realities of an entire nation are hidden; she gives us cues about the oppression of a nation and the oppression of a gender. This turns the story of the film into an intense narrative. Despite its profound content, however, Arslan's documentary shows signs of technical limitations. Her stylistic approach is affected by the film's small budget and by having only a small crew, consisting of one or two camerapersons, and limited equipment.

The deterritorialized style resulting from having a very limited budget enables many female filmmakers of Women's New Cinema to produce accented films. Preferring collective and interstitial mode of production, Berke Baş, Melisa Önel, Hatice Kamer, and Bingöl Elmas are some filmmakers who produce their films and adapt the "aesthetics of hunger."[6] Despite encouraging more women

Figure 3.3 Kurdish women telling their story. The still is from *A Fatal Dress: Polygamy*.

to produce their own content freely, it is important to ask if the reason why this style is mainly adapted by women and/or Kurdish directors is that women/Kurds are less supported financially than their male/Turkish counterparts.[7]

Borders

As liminal subjects positioned at the border, accented directors make their films drawing upon biographical crossing experiences (Naficy 2001, 32). We can observe this "border consciousness" in the accented films of Women's New Cinema. In *I Flew You Stayed*, for instance, despite finding it quite dangerous for herself as well as the camera and camerawoman (Fontini 2024b, 6), Arslan crossed several geographical borders including the one between Turkey and Iraq during her journey to seek her father's footprints. Unlike the territorial journey, in her psychological journey, she reveals familial relationships; she exposes the "secrets" of her family by questioning her personal life in front of the cameras and opening her memories to debate. In this way, she crosses the borders between the private and the public by making what is supposed to remain private public; she "leaks." Talking about her private life within a public medium also lends a feminist emphasis to the content of her film. Revealing the memories of a Kurdish family, she also crosses the borders between ideologies and histories. The personal journey of a girl examining her father's life disrupts the hegemonic historical discourse. In this sense, Women's New Cinema creates a counter-history consisting of the memories of the vulnerable communities.

Arslan's stylistic preferences also offer several border-crossing examples. Her stylistic signature that uses the conventions of documentary and fiction together strengthens her authorial statement while blurring the borders of genres. It also fails the expectations of the audience who are accustomed to the codes of classical narrations. The film's defamiliarizing, self-reflexive style performs a critique of the mainstream, dominant cinema. Arslan's presence in the film as director and actor breaks down the distinction between the protagonist and the filmmaker. She also worked as the scriptwriter, co-producer, and co-editor of the documentary. As a co-producer, she was involved in the financing and screening stages of the film. Her style of working underlines the artisanal mode of production and also blurs the borders of division of labor, both of which are shared features of accented films.

Crossing borders not only inside the films but also geographically, women's cinema is evaluated as "the cinema of the world" by recent scholarship (White 2015). Arslan's documentary, along with other accented films of Women's New Cinema, are screened internationally, which makes them transnationally accessible, proving the argument of recent scholarship. This also underlines that Women's New Cinema is an international cinema due to the way the films are funded, screened, distributed, positioned at festivals, and viewed cross-culturally. *I Flew You Stayed* (2012) targets a diverse group of audiences, such as the Kurdish community, as accented audiences. The film was well received and was officially selected to screen at prestigious international film festivals such as the 1st Amed International Film Festival, the 1st Van Gölü International Film Festival, the 2nd Dersim International Human Rights Film Festival, and the 7th Sinemardin International Film Festival (Mizgin M. Arslan 2023). "'Collective enunciation' in which filmmakers and audiences are conjoined by their membership in communities" and collective reception also blurs the borders between producers and consumers. It evaluates the audience as creative readers (Naficy 2001, 45). In addition to its accented audiences, the film has been officially selected to screen in Turkish film festivals; the 45th SİYAD, the 5th Documentarist Istanbul Documentary Days; 16th Flying Broom International Women's Film Festival; the 18th London Turkish Film Festival; the 7th Boston Turkish Documentary and Short Film Festival; the 66th Cannes Turkish Stand; and the 63rd Berlin Turkish Stand (Mizgin M. Arslan 2023). Interestingly, the film is recognized as a Turkish production internationally, which reflects the ambivalent nationality of the film. It is important to highlight that Arslan as a Kurdish person was unable to enter the Kurdish region where her father's grave is because she holds a Turkish passport, which makes the nationality of the filmmaker ironically ambivalent as well. These samples also provide strong criticism of the status of the Kurdish nation.

I also see the experience of border crossing in Arslan's choice of language. The film shows linguistic liminality. Although when the characters speak Kurdish, Turkish subtitles are included, we hear some Turkish conversations—accented ones—without any Kurdish subtitles. The reason might be learning Turkish is required in the institutional educational system and Turkey does not offer education in any other language but Turkish. So, a Kurdish person watching the film would understand the spoken Turkish without subtitles but a Turkish person would need subtitles for the parts in Kurdish. This proves the dominance of Turkish structure and its oppression of other cultures. Additionally, speaking Kurdish in a film within a Turkish context always indicates more than just speaking a language; it always goes beyond its diegetic meaning. It means that now it is possible to talk in Kurdish because sometimes it was/is not (Çiftçi 2009, 269). As stated by Naficy (2001, 24, 122), the accented filmmaker's insistence on using her native language to the detriment of broader festival screening can be read as her desire to keep the bond between herself and her native culture. In Arslan's case, the reason might be her desire to preserve and maintain her culture. Or else as mentioned by the scholar, and author Bahar Şimşek:

> It is important to build a festival audience that understands and speaks Kurdish. This is a new aesthetic plane that can liberate films and their audiences from the pressure of explaining their troubles to the "master" and convincing them, or holding a mirror to trauma. In other words, I think the possibility of Kurdish cinema as a more dynamic structure without breaking its ties with Kurdishness and culture might be present here (Şimşek, Çiçek, and Koçer 2023).

However, whether to speak the Kurdish or Turkish language is a very complex issue in practice. For instance, Suncem Koçer who is the co-producer and set photographer in Kazım Öz's *Demsala dawi: Sewaxan / The Last Season: Shawaks* (2009) says that speaking in Turkish in that Kurdish film set was not ideal because when they spoke in Turkish, others started responding in Turkish and it ruined the authenticity (Şimşek, Çiçek, and Koçer 2023). On the other hand, young Kurdish women on the set were speaking in Turkish during the breaks so that their elders and men could not understand them. According to Koçer, speaking in Turkish for these young women was a way to "construct a counter space to their family elders," and "an escape from them" (2023). The issue here is not always an ideological one; thinking on a subjective level, the choice of language gains different political meanings.

Besides linguistic liminality, *I Flew You Stayed* crosses the borders between ideologies and histories through spoiling the coherence of the official history. Arslan's search, her attempt to illuminate her personal past going back almost thirty years in time, triggers the Kurdish people's memories of the struggle between Kurdish and Turkish. We listen to the catastrophic memories of the previous generation—how families were split and torture experienced by Kurdish men and women. For marginalized and (de)territorialized people, "collective memory, rather than official history, is of crucial importance" (Gabriel 1990, 402). In a similar way, in Baş's *Hush!*, the "unofficial" story of Nahide is told that rejects the official discourse on the events of 1915; in Gündoğan's *Two Locks of Hair: The Lost Girls of Dersim* and *Unburied in The Past—The Missing Girls of The Dersim*, viewers witness the life story of Emoş, which contradicts the hegemonic historical discourse on the Dersim massacre. In *Waiting for the Clouds*, by showing the forced migration of Greek families through Ayşe/Eleni's story, Ustaoğlu represents a personal but at the same time collective trauma and invalidation of an identity. As seen, the accented films of Women's New Cinema create a counter-memory through replacing the official records with the memory itself. This enables the writing of an alternative historiography.

While analyzing these films, Umut Tümay Arslan brings another perspective to the discussion:

> Feminism can only exist by recognizing the heterogeneity and antagonisms between women's histories. A look that is perceptive of the power structures might mean to be able to see the power struggle over women's bodies. There is no single basis for domination; being forced to take off the headscarf and to cover naked parts of the body can also be seen as forcing people to forget a denied violent past, a language and identity, and the heterogeneous memory of the geography. That's why the documentary *Two Locks of Hair: The Lost Girls of Dersim* (Nezahat Gündoğan, 2010) or movies like *Waiting for the Clouds* (Yeşim Ustaoğlu, 2003) or *Dust Cloth* (Ahu Öztürk) are examples of establishing solidarities not despite but with the antagonisms between the histories of women from Turkey. These are the films that make us think about the possibilities and make us pursue women's cinema, not the female gaze. (U. T. Arslan 2022c)

As I will explore further in this chapter, the accentedness of Women's New Cinema means to develop a gaze that is "power-sensitive" rather than a "pluralist" (such as racially sensitive or gender-specific) gaze (Haraway 1988, 589). This is another type of border consciousness, the one which understands that power structures such as racism, misogyny, and homophobia are not separate from each other but they are extensions of each other functioning together. Recognizing this, Women's New Cinema establishes possible connections between different womanhoods.

In addition to contradicting the hegemonic historical discourse and providing us with alternative solidarities, the accented feature of Women's New Cinema disrupts the linearity of time. *I Flew You Stayed*, for example, creates an ambiguity through moving from present to past. As well as listening to the memories of the witnesses, we see many photographs and letters (Figure 3.4) and listen to Arslan's father's voice played from a cassette. The images, sounds and characters trigger the private "sense memories" (Marks 1994, 258) of the exilic audience; that is, through these images, the accented audience goes back to the places, people, sounds, tastes—the home they left behind. However, on this "back-to-their-roots" journey, what the characters find most of the time is dispossession. In *Unburied in The Past—The Missing Girls of The Dersim*, Emoş goes back to the village where she was born after seventy-four years' away; what she finds are houses and churches that are turned into ruins and people who turn into ghosts. In these scenes, what we feel is an "absence." Rather than making us think that somebody once existed, these techniques make us feel that they are currently disappearing (Neyzi 2013, 106). Reconstructing the presence of the past from the present "absence," these films crack the time of the nation, and recognize dispossession as a slow violence.

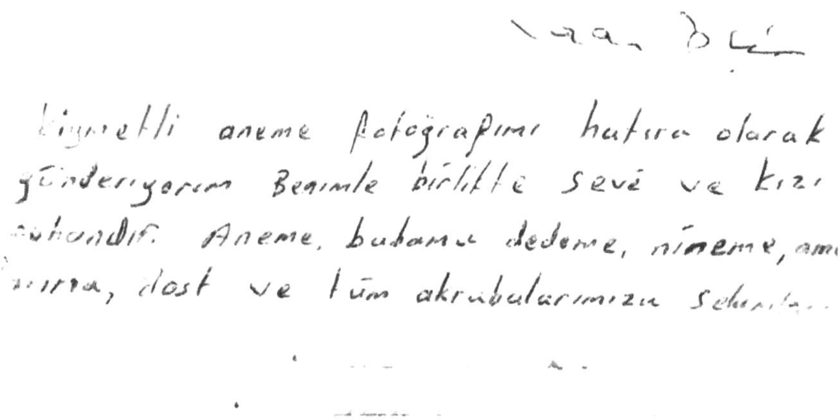
aneme fotoğrafımı hatıra olarak
gönderiyorum ... birlikte ... ve kızı
Aneme, babama, dedeme, nineme,
dost ve tüm akrabalarımıza

Figure 3.4 A letter from *I Flew You Stayed.*

Arslan's narrative turns the concept of time into a hybrid one; the experience of border crossing in this sense happens within the temporality of the film. In *I Flew You Stayed*, she focuses on the past, but examines its effects on the present moment, now. According to the scholar and author Özgür Çiçek, "the most exciting point" regarding films like *I Flew You Stayed* "is to capture personal stories and details of daily life within all this layered and historical political baggage, to enter into the present while continuing to question the past, or to feel and make the audience feel the depth in the present" (Şimşek, Çiçek, and Koçer 2023). While bringing past memories into present, Arslan's questionings also create present memories and emotions. She transfers these present memories to the previous generation when she talks to the elders about how she feels and her current experience. This creates cyclic time and a cyclic memory. Unlike in classical narratives where time flows in a linear manner, Arslan uses a non-linear, cyclic flow. In this sense, she subverts the codes of mainstream narratives.

The Principles of Accented Feminism and Accented Feminist Cinema

As Naficy's accented cinema model lacks a gender dimension in its imagery of nation, identity, and belonging, it is inadequate to explain some of the major features of accented *female* filmmakers from Turkey. To be able to understand their experiences, I integrate a gender dimension into my perspective and discuss accented cinema in a broader context. For this purpose, I propose the term "accented feminism." Accented feminism provides an alternative to the term "third world" (e.g., "third world woman," "third world feminism," "post-third-worldist feminism"). Terminological constructions using "third world" imply the existence of a first and second world from which the third world emerges. Such formulations make the third world dependent on the first world to exist, while the hierarchical order of the worlds indicates cultural, economic and social distances among these geographies, signing the first one as more advanced and more civilized than the others. The term "third world" also groups many countries together with "oversimplified similarities," "reinforcing existing economic, cultural, and ideological hierarchies" (Mohanty 1991b, 74–5).

Accented feminism problematizes the notion of nation and it "break[s] away from the narrative of the 'nation' as a unified entity so as to articulate a contextualized history for women in specific geographies of identity" (Shohat 2003, 52). Lazreg states,

> Underlying the struggle of Western feminists is the assumption that they belong to perfectible societies . . . This seldom recognized fact allows Western feminists to perceive themselves as fundamentally different from Other women whom they tend to define as 'oppressed' and in need of liberation. (2000, 31)

These Western feminists cannot connect with "other" women (Black women, Muslim women, Middle Eastern women) without divesting themselves of white supremacist thinking. They cannot give up the idea that they are better, smarter, even kinder and more civilized than the "other" women.[8] In return, many artists, academics and intellectuals marginalized as such see themselves as "lacking." As Pratibha Parmar says,

> Images play a crucial role in defining and controlling the political and social power to which both individuals and marginalized groups have access. The deeply ideological nature of imagery determines not only how other people think about us but how we think about ourselves. (1990, 116)

Using the power of images, accented feminist artists change how others see "other" women and how we see ourselves. They make us come closer to ourselves and embrace our existence. In this regard, the act of loving ourselves transforms into political resistance.[9]

Rejecting the Eurocentric image of a universal "womanhood," accented feminism also formulates a film critique. Accented feminist film critique intervenes with the tradition of feminist film theory. The first arguments that set the major principles of feminist film theory were shaped in the West by feminist film theorists influenced by second wave feminism at the beginning of the 1970s. The birth of new disciplines such as Film Studies and Women's Studies, new approaches in structural linguistics and the continental European theories of ideology, semiotics, and psychoanalysis enriched the debates on women's cinema and contributed to the context of feminist film theory. Theorists such as Claire Johnston (1973) and Laura Mulvey ([1975] 1999) began to criticize female representation while the concepts of other disciplines such as psychoanalysis and semiotics allowed them to analyze the construction of pleasure and subjectivity. Yet their dismissal of the racial and national conditions that produce differences among women led to the construction of a monolithic womanhood. Prominent film journals of the 1970s, such as *Screen* "screened out black and Third World film practices, confining itself to a narrowly Eurocentric canon" (Kobena 1994, 56). "Failing to take into account how racial, ethnic, class, or sexual antagonisms and inequalities were articulated with gendered power relations could lead feminist film theory to 'reinforce white middle-class values'" (U. T. Arslan 2022c; hooks 1992). Their disregard for place-specific context might hinder our ability to "argue for specific forms of resistance in relation to diverse forms of oppression" (Shohat 2001, 291). In rejecting the Eurocentric concept of a universal womanhood and including locational facts in the discussion, accented feminist theorists can deconstruct the white feminist film theory created in the first world metropolises. For the remainder of this paper, I will develop a critique that deconstructs the white feminist film theory which can also contribute to the scholarship that involves the arguments of race and ethnicity in feminist discussions.

In the final section, I will adapt the approach of Suner in order to evaluate the documentaries of Arslan. Suner adapts the accented feminist perspectives to the discussions of accented cinema. She develops a "critical stance vis-à- vis patriarchal ideology and the prejudices in hegemonic Western feminism against the Middle East and Islam" (Suner 2007, 54). Analyzing an accented film *Waiting for the Clouds*, she criticizes the hegemony of Turkish identity over Greek identity and the prejudices of Western feminism towards the Middle Eastern artist. Adapting Suner's approach, I will evaluate the documentaries of Arslan in the next section. I will include a critique of patriarchal ideology as well as the prejudices of hegemonic Western feminism against the Middle East and Islam. In my context, however, the criticism is against both the home and host nations and the local and Western feminisms. Arslan also highlights the political struggle of Kurdish women while criticizing the first world Eurocentric feminism and the hegemonic Turkish/state feminism[10] which is in alignment with official national discourse. In this regard, she enlarges the realm of the accented feminist film critique and enables us not only to criticize "the other" but also confront our own selves.

Decolonizing Feminist Discourse

Accented feminism makes a simultaneous criticism not only of different forms of oppression but also of feminist hegemony (Kaplan and Grewal 1999). I now analyze Arslan's documentary to discuss how Women's New Cinema breaks formed and fixed notions through bringing a two-sided critique: while criticizing the nationalist feudal structure of the Kurdish nation, Arslan simultaneously criticizes the Turkish nationalism and hegemonic Eurocentric and Turkish/state feminisms.

Arslan deconstructs national spaces and identities within her film by contradicting a common fantasy: "Islamic women of the Middle East are typically seen as victims of religion, patriarchy, tradition, and poverty in the West. Women artists from the same region are expected to testify to this presumed condition" (Amireh and Majaj quoted in Suner 2007, 65–6). Arslan does not fulfill the expectations of a "Middle Eastern, Muslim, third-world" artist by daring to have a journey by herself to discover her personal story and claiming her memories back; she creates her story by herself and she owns the agency. The director also "fails" to meet common expectations; she centers her family in *I Flew You Stayed* rather than the state's oppression or Kurdish traditions.

Focusing on the relationship of exile and culture, Trinh T. Minh-ha says

> The Afrikaners are prompt in saying "You can take a black man from the bush, but you can't take the bush from the black man." Since you can't take the bush from the black man, it is the bush that is consistently given back to him. (1991, 69)

Colonizers tend to treat marginalized people based on a monolithic lens. In a similar manner, it is the one-way womanhood that is consistently given back to "other" women. The Eurocentric universalizing of womanhood assumes an already formed, coherent group with identical needs, desires and objections who needs liberation. In *I Flew You Stayed*, Arslan tells us her personal story, which is intertwined with the story of her mother. In Arslan's first documentary, *A Fatal Dress: Polygamy*, the director creates a space where Kurdish women tell their personal stories. In this way, Arslan reveals the multiple and complex existences of Kurdish women that spoil the assumptions and expectations of the West.

As Arslan refuses to produce knowledge "about" Kurdish women, she manages to tell their stories without resorting to Eurocentric ideas. Particularly in *A Fatal Dress: Polygamy*, she problematizes the tradition of polygamy by showing that the patriarchal, feudal codes of Kurdish society are not a part of Kurdish culture. Therefore, her storytelling does not become another form of oppression in which being Muslim and Kurd become entangled. This, however, is where the problem gets complicated. Ahmed explains:

> When we speak of violence directed against us [people of color], we know how quickly that violence can be racialized; how racism will explain that violence as an expression of culture, which is how racism and religion become entangled. Violence would then again be assumed to originate with outsiders. Some forms of violence become cultural, and other forms of violence remain individual and idiosyncratic: some of this distinction is racism . . . We must still tell these stories of violence because of how quickly that violence is concealed and reproduced. We must always tell them with care. But it is risky: when they are taken out of hands, they can become another form of beating. (2017b, 72)

Deploying a double-sided critique, Arslan does not produce a racially sensitive or a gender-specific gaze, but she develops a gaze vulnerable to hegemonies or, as named by Haraway, a "power-sensitive" gaze (1988, 589). In this way, she manages to reject both the feudal structure of Kurdish communities and the understanding that patriarchy is the tradition of Kurdish culture. What her film does for us, as female viewers, is that it

> allows us to look at women and ourselves with eyes that we did not have before or did not know we had, but that we can now call our own, that is, it allows us to see the boundaries and distinctions called difference in a different way, it opens this space. (U. T. Arslan 2022c)

Deconstructing the Heterosexual and Masculine Nationalist Discourse and Constructing an Anti-colonial and Feminist Discourse

To understand the cinema of accented *female* directors from Turkey, it is necessary to also consider how they deal with colonialism and nationalism in their films. The accented female directors of Women's New Cinema decolonize feminist discourse and deconstruct the heterosexual and masculine nationalist discourse which is the traditional discourse of accented films. As explained by Shohat:

> Third-Worldist films often favored the generic and gendered space of heroic confrontations, whether set in the streets, the casbah, the mountains, or the jungle. The minimal presence of women corresponded to the place assigned to women both in the anti-colonialist revolutions and within Third-Worldist

> discourse, leaving women's homebound struggles unacknowledged. Women occasionally carried the bombs, as in *The Battle of Algiers*, but only in the name of a "Nation." More often, women were made to carry the "burden" of national allegory: the woman dancing with the flag in *The Battle of Algiers*, the Argentinian prostitute whose image is underscored by the national anthem in *La Hora de Los Hornos* (*The Hour of the Furnaces*), the mestiza journalist in Cubagua, embodying the Venezuelan nation; or else the symbolic women are scapegoated as personifications of imperialism, for example, the allegorical "whore of Babylon" figure in Rocha's films. Gender contradictions have been subordinated to anti-colonial struggle: women were expected to "wait their turn." (2003, 59)

In Arslan's documentaries, women do not wait their turn: they occupy the space of the protagonist and speak of a different nation and belonging. In this way, Arslan creates a national imagery where women are independent and empowered. Similarly, Ayşe/Eleni in *Waiting for the Clouds* dares to remember her past and embrace her real identity after decades, deciding to go from her small village in Turkey to Thessaloniki to find her brother. Emoş in *Unburied in The Past—The Missing Girls of The Dersim* visits her village after spending a lifetime away from it and finds her cousin and her memories amongst the ruins left after the massacre. In *Me and Nuri Bala*, we watch Esmeray's story of realizing herself as a transsexual Kurdish artist after struggling with the heteronormative and national codes of her community and the Turkish state. The female characters in these accented films depict a different kind of being and belonging.

In an interview about Kurdish cinema, Şimşek says:

> Discussing Kurdish cinema only around the topics of borders, statelessness and death creates a comfort zone. This comfort zone is the work of a regime of truth that reduces Kurdishness to victimization, its justness, truth, and aesthetics to its victimization. The carriers of this regime are the male director, the male protagonist, the weak female body that has been made sick or aged, the trauma narratives in which patriarchy is reconstructed around the family, and a kind of over-determined aesthetics that adorn these narratives. (Şimşek, Çiçek, and Koçer 2023)

Arslan, as a Kurdish woman, focuses on the intersection of being a Kurd and a woman in her films. Her not serving the "regime of truth" reducing "Kurdishness/Kurdish womanhood to victimization" is quite crucial for Kurdish cinema. Another striking example comes from Ahu Öztürk's *Dust Cloth*. As analyzed by Umut Tümay Arslan:

> In the film, we cannot concentrate only on the Kurdish issue, only the women's issue, and only the class issue. When you take one, the movie forces you to take the other one after it. The film, which embodies the historical differences and heterogeneity between women, does not assign a single image or a fixed position about being a woman, being a Kurd or a domestic worker. (U. T. Arslan, 2022c)

As mentioned by Umut Tümay Arslan, the films of Women's New Cinema are aware of inequalities based on colonialism, racism, and capitalism. While confronting us with them, they attempt to imagine different kinds of womanhood, nationality, and belonging. *A Fatal Dress: Polygamy* provides another such example. In the documentary, Arslan narrates the effects of polygamy on women. In employing parallel editing, she critiques the patriarchal discourse misusing religious references to confirm men's actions. This perspective seems like contradicting the expectations of the national Kurdish cinema because Kurdish films are mainly expected to depict the oppression Kurdish society receives from the state. In this documentary, Arslan creates a space for the women to speak for themselves and criticize the tradition of polygamy with anecdotes from their own lives. It is "a challenge to the discourse of stranger danger, which assumes that [oppression] originates outside of home" (Ahmed 2017b, 72). This critique strengthens the feminist statement of her documentaries. In other words, Arslan constructs another layer of critique in this documentary: feminist decolonization within the imagery of nation. By carrying personal and familial experiences into the public in both of her documentaries, she also spoils the idea of belonging; belonging to a family that expects the family members to keep the secrets within the family, and belonging to a nation that requires the citizens to keep the national secrets within the nation. In *I Flew You Stayed*, on the other hand, she problematizes the attitude of her family by questioning her own mother on her decision to take her son with her but leave her daughter behind. In a broader sense, she questions the role Kurdish patriarchal beliefs have played in her mother's decision: to take him with them but leave her behind.

At this point, it is also important to mention that Arslan has received strong criticism from her audience (Fontini 2024b, 11). Representation of the community is a highly sensitive issue within accented films (Naficy 2001, 64–5). As Arslan shows the dreadful impact of Kurdish patriarchy and feudalism on women, including herself, male members of the community and some members of her family have become defensive and criticized the director's depiction of Kurdish men as cruel, and even ask her to stop the film's screening online. This internal censorship attempt has failed.

Arslan's discourse on nation is closely related to anti-colonial and feminist discourses. While stating her personal situation and revealing the personal stories of Kurdish people in her film, she implies that the nation-state is the cause of families falling apart, living in immigration camps, and Kurdish children not being able to receive education in their mother tongue. Despite it being illegal, young girls are forced to get married as child brides and men can take second or third wives. This shows the failure of official institutions. By showing what is there, Arslan shows what is not there. These situations make it clear that legal rules are not implemented in some parts of Turkey, resulting in some people being less of a citizen, especially if the person in question is a Kurd and a woman. In this sense, her films recognize not only the violence but also the violence created by its refusal (see Sharpe 2023, 38).

Including gender in the imagery of nation and race in the imagery of feminism provides the director and the audience with a better perspective that questions inherited realities and truths. However, the discourse Arslan constructs on gender on the basis for equal rights is not only related to Kurdish women but also to Turkish women because the freedom of Kurdish women relates to the freedom of Turkish women. Additionally, the liberation struggle she indicates is inclusive of Kurdish men and women because without free Kurdish women, we cannot imagine a free Kurdish nation. As stated by Mohanty, "It is not the oppression, race or gender that prepare the bases for a struggle but rather how we react to the oppressive forces, the oppressive alliance is the common context of struggle" (1991a, 4, 7). And it is a political alliance that is established not despite but with these inherent differences.

By being inspired by anti-colonial and feminist discourses, other accented female filmmakers of Women's New Cinema construct female characters in ways responsive to this discourse. Unlike the previous decades when most women's films have represented white, Western, middle-class liberal feminism through putting "a singular focus on gender as a basis for equal rights," accented feminist films "focus on gender in relation to race and/or class as part of a broader liberation struggle" (Mohanty 1991a, 11). The representation of Nahide in *Hush!*, for instance, does not solely reflect the meaning of being a woman or being an Armenian but being an Armenian woman in Turkey. It is a story of a young Armenian girl, Nahide, who is adopted by a Turkish family during the events of 1915 and at the same time it is also the story of Nahide's being the second wife of a Turkish man. The narrative is about her losing some parts of her Armenian identity, her roots and her experiences as being someone's second wife. Similarly, in *Unburied in The Past—The Missing Girls of The Dersim*, Emoş's story is about her losing her Kurdish-Alevi identity and at the same time, about her girlhood experience of being sent to a military family where she serves as a handmaiden. In *Me and Nuri*

Bala, Esmeray's life story not only represents the lives of transsexuals in Turkey but also depicts what it means to be a Kurdish transsexual. The film shows how Esmeray struggles as a transsexual against the transphobic, masculine codes of the Turkish state and the transphobic, feudal codes of the Kurdish community. These female representations clearly show how national and institutional identities are deconstructed in Women's New Cinema.

Conclusion: Accented Imagery, "How the World Might be Otherwise"[11]

In *Wayward Lives, Beautiful Experiments* (2020), Saidiya Hartman defines the young women of early twentieth-century America as "radical thinkers who tirelessly imagined other ways to live and never failed to consider how the world might be otherwise" (xv). She says:

> The book describes the as if—as if we were free, as if a beautiful life were possible. It is earned by so much loss and destruction, blood and tears. It's not an easy celebration. It's not a vitalist rejoicing, but an extended meditation on the impossible and the necessary: *what does it mean to even imagine that life is possible* and to want something like the good life when life itself cannot be taken for granted; when one lives under the threat of death; when captivity is the prevailing scheme? How does one live in that context? (Hartman quoted in Bulley 2020; original emphasis)

Similarly, Mizgin Müjde Arslan and the other accented female filmmakers of Women's New Cinema are radical thinkers who imagine how the world might be otherwise. Providing sights of vulnerable others, they challenge the hegemonic historic discourse, offer an alternative collective memory, and consider other ways to live. They tell the audience the stories of "other" women making life possible despite racism, hegemonic statism, hegemonic feminism and patriarchy. Through problematizing multiple faces of oppression (hegemonic Turkish nationalism, hegemonic feminism, and patriarchal Kurdish feudalism), the accented feminist films within Women's New Cinema compose a counter-discourse and create oppositional agency. In this sense, the "accented imagery" created by the accented female filmmakers of Women's New Cinema transforms what cinema is in contemporary Turkey.

Women's New Cinema, with its accented features, invents another vision. It does not simply represent a diverse population or recognize the "other" but imagines that a dignified life is possible. On the tenth-year commemoration of Hrant Dink, Rakel Dink mentions a similar point: "The important thing is not just to live together, but to live equally and happily; and to live honorably and freely" (R. Dink, 2017). The accented possibility women's cinema aims to create is quite similar to the vision Dink was hoping for all.

Notes

1. A version of this chapter was published by *Feminist Media Studies* (Fontini, 2022b), copyright Taylor & Francis, available online: https://www.tandfonline.com/doi/full/10.1080/14680777.2022.2048046.
2. In this story, there are words like 'uncle,' 'brother,' and 'son.' It does not mean that these people are relatives. In Turkey, we call each other with these names because of kinship we feel toward each other as community.
3. To commemorate Dink, please visit (Hrant Dink Foundation 2007; Oğur and Gasparyan 2013).
4. Drawing the concept from Gilles Deleuze and Felix Guattari's "minor literature", many other scholars have recently been working on the exilic/diasporic subjects living in the West (Suner 2006b, 363). Coining the term "intercultural cinema", Laura U. Marks (2000) mainly works on Asian, Latin American, Caribbean, African, and Middle Eastern filmmakers (including videomakers), while Will Higbee and Song Hwee Lim (2010) discuss the diasporic and postcolonial cinemas with the concepts of transnationalism. Books such as *European Cinema in Motion: Migrant and Diasporic Film in Contemporary Europe* (Berghahn and Sternberg 2010) and *Screening Strangers: Migration and Diaspora in Contemporary European Cinema* (Loshitzky 2010) provide multidimensional perspectives while thinking on migrant and diasporic cinemas. See also (Kobena 1994) and (Gabriel 1990).
5. See "*Ez Firiyam Tu Mayi Li Cih* (*I Flew You Stayed/Ben Uçtum Sen Kaldın*): An Example of Domestic Ethnography" (Koçer 2016) for an extended understanding of its ethnographic features.
6. With this term, Glauber Rocha ([1965] 2019) argues that third cinema should reflect the "essence" of third world societies—hunger in its style through adapting imperfect stylistic features.
7. The national funding system and the reasons why female filmmakers are supported less financially are discussed in detail in Chapter 6.
8. In her book *Black Looks: Race and Representation*, bell hooks says that white people "were often unable to let go the idea that whites are somehow better, smarter, more likely to be intellectuals, and even that they were kinder than black folks" (1992, 10). While it cannot be denied that Black women, Muslim women and Middle Eastern women cannot be identified as an identical group, as far as being the "other" to hegemonic Western feminists, their problems and the struggles are similar.
9. Here I adapted hook's comparison between white supremacist thinking and Black people to my context. In her essay, hooks offers loving Blackness as political resistance (1992, 10–11).
10. It is important to understand the feminist genealogy in Turkey to define the hegemonic Turkish/state feminism and the accented ones. A group of women such as Nezihe Muhiddin, Zabel Yaseyan, Hayganuş Mark vocalized their pro-feminist

demands (i.e., autonomy and equality for Greek, Armenian, Jewish, Turkish, Arab, and Kurdish women) in the early Turkish/late Ottoman period. However, the movement of these pioneer women was hindered by the state. The official history narrates Mustafa Kemal Atatürk (the first president of Turkey) as the leader/father 'giving' the rights to women/daughters (see Zihnioglu 2003; Bilal and Ekmekçioğlu 2006). Kemalist state ideology constructed a figure of woman who deserved her rights insomuch as she worked in building the nation-state.

"From the 1960s to 1980s, women took active roles in Marxist social movement. This leftist opposition evaluated feminism as the ideology of the bourgeois class, the figure of woman was constructed, again, as revolutionaries and genderless. From the 1980s on (starting with the 1980 Turkish coup d'état), the state got more and more authoritarian. But the same period witnessed the emergence of a new feminist movement whose aim was to deconstruct the patriarchal and militarist tradition and bring a new understanding to social opposition. Effected by and effecting the feminist wave, new and diverse social movements (such as LGBTI+, ecologist, anti-militarist, anarchist, Kurdish, Armenian, and on) emerged. During the 1990s, due to the continuing state oppression, these oppositional ideologies had to form alliances. Such interactions transformed the ideologies enabling the development of new, diverse and intersectional discourses. Feminist movement, the most diverse group of all the social opposition, shaped itself as pacifist, anti-militarist, multiracial, and pro-LGBTI+. In 2000s, with the rise of a new authoritarianism, Turkey has undergone a new national and militarist/paramilitarist era. The feminist movement has been trying to protect itself and resist against a conservative Turkey which left the Istanbul Convention. The JDP government continue assigning new traditional roles to women" (Selek, 2021). I take transfeminism, Kurdish feminism, jineolojî/ jineology, Armenian feminism and queer feminism as accented feminism within the Turkish context. And against the diversity of accented feminism, I identify two hegemonic feminisms: the Turkish national/state feminism and the Eurocentric feminism.

11. Here I am repeating the statement of Saidiya Hartman (2020, xv).

Chapter 4

"The Master's Tools Will Never Dismantle the Master's House": The Political Aesthetics of Women's New Cinema[1]

It was 1976 when Silvia Bovenschen asked if there is a feminine aesthetic (Bovenschen 1977). Forty-four years later, I posed the same question to Zeynep Dadak, a mid-career director of Women's New Cinema and one of the directors of *The Blue Wave*. Her response was:

> It's favourable to describe a specific cinematic language as female within the patriarchal discourse. If a man writes a scenario, they say it's mathematical. If a woman writes a scenario, they say it's like a piece of lacework. We don't need those descriptions. But what shapes my outlook on the world is, of course, feminism. I feel like a part of the feminist struggle. You know, my critical ideas, my opinions were formed by what I read, and did; these definitely affect my own work. (Dadak quoted in Fontini, 2020; personal communication)

Dadak says she, and therefore her work, is affected by feminist critique, but she is against using the terms to stereotype the kinds of work made by women. Like Dadak, the aim of the arguments presented in this chapter is not to understand if I can name the aesthetic strategies used by the directors of Women's New Cinema as feminine or not but to understand the various stylistic strategies practiced by the female directors of Women's New Cinema and the politics, poetics and ethics behind them. Drawing upon a much earlier feminist critique, the term "political aesthetics" is reawakened to discuss those many strategies. The political here is not about being morally true or politically correct but an umbrella term embracing those various practices.[2]

To launch the discussion, I analyze the characteristics of the film *The Blue Wave*, because the aesthetic tactics adapted by Zeynep Dadak and Merve Kayan, the directors of that film, are representative of the trends I aim to identify. They choose to tell an "ordinary" story without using the codes of classical narration such as identification with the main character, catharsis, and a closed ending. They prefer dedramatization as their filmic style, which is signified through the repeated failure to create tension and/or catharsis and the promotion of solidarity and sisterhood. Shohini Chaudhuri and Howard Finn's (2003) term "open image" helps me to develop this argument. Although Chaudhuri and Finn use the term as an apolitical aesthetic form to evaluate the New Iranian Cinema (2003, 38), I change and enlarge the concept by adding political and feminist values to it. By comparing the stylistic preferences of Dadak and Kayan with the codes of conventional narrative films, I discuss how Women's New Cinema challenges the stylistic norms of classical mainstream films. Evaluating the anti-oppressive, feminist, and ethical aesthetic strategies adopted by the contemporary female filmmakers of Women's New Cinema, this chapter explores how Women's New Cinema subverts, deconstructs, or destabilizes the hegemonic, sexist language, enabling us to see the world with new eyes, to see *her* ways of living.

Open Image as Everyday Image

In their influential essay "The Open Image: Poetic Realism and the New Iranian Cinema," Chaudhuri and Finn evaluate the image not as a reflection of contemporary Iranian social reality but as an apolitical aesthetic form; they identify the open image not as a reflection of the extraordinary but with the order of the everyday (2003, 38). The everyday here refers to the depiction of the mundane represented by "understated acting" and "dedramatization" (2003, 41). Understanding the image as an everyday image not as an extraordinary one illuminates the aesthetics of *The Blue Wave* too. I will now briefly tell the story of the film and then unfold the characteristics of the image.

The Blue Wave narrates a young woman's coming-of-age story. After returning from her summer holiday, Deniz finds that everything has stayed the same in her small hometown. She meets with her friends Gül, Esra, and Perin. While catching up, the girls tell each other about their summer holidays, their lovelives, and the stress of their upcoming university exam. Right at the beginning of the movie, we learn that Deniz likes her teacher, Fırat, but she also has an interest in her school friend, Kaya. Deniz and her friends spend their days listening to music, smoking, drinking, and talking about life. Deniz changes the major she wants to study at university but Fırat wants to intervene in the situation. In the meantime, Deniz does not feel comfortable getting closer to her teacher and she starts to distance herself from him. The ambiance of the city reflects Deniz and her friends' uncertain and uneasy feelings about the future. There are frequent water, electricity, and gas cuts and there is a shortage of stock of products in the market, which causes uneasiness and uncertainty for the local people. Meanwhile, Deniz and Kaya have their first sexual experience together. Deniz tells her friends about this experience on an excursion. The movie ends when Deniz and her friends say goodbye to Kaya, who is moving to another city to study.

When considering the narrative of *The Blue Wave*, I found it difficult to summarize as there is no single particular inciting incident that sets the story in motion. Rather, the film is made up of sequences that illustrate "the dull, banal commonplaces of everyday living" (Chaudhuri and Finn 2003, 41). The major point emphasized in the film is not Deniz's romantic relationship with Fırat or Kaya, nor her relationship with her family; indeed, there is no one major point at all but rather several minor points that occur throughout the narrative. They are Deniz's first sexual experience, her disappointment, her relationship with her family and friends, her expectations, and the new decisions she makes, all of which she experiences as a part of her daily and ordinary life. In this sense, the film is composed of many daily encounters, life happenings, and mood swings. As Dadak and Kayan mention:

> When so many things that have no value in everyday life come together, an incredible movie can emerge. For example, Agnès Varda's and Chris Marker's films are like that. A strange poem emerges from the combination of events and people who have no hierarchical value in themselves. This poem does not necessarily result from the image itself being a terrific image, but from the combination of a whole bunch of less important things that we just talked about . . . This accumulation is exactly where our story of growing up in the country comes together with this film. When you look back, an event that seemed like the most important issue in the world that day turns into something that will not be considered the next day. (2014)

Other films from Women's New Cinema that use moments from the everyday to construct their narratives include *The Blue Wave*, *Present Tense*, *Motherland*, *Zephyr*, *Lifelong*, *Dust Cloth*, *Clair Obscur*, and *Something Useful*.

Another characteristic of the everyday image is its emphasis on the emotional effect it creates on the character. Maya Deren coined the term "vertical investigation" to describe this particularity in women's cinema. To her, women's films are "concerned in a sense not with what is occurring, but with what it feels like or what it means" (Deren quoted in Knight 1992, 123). The emphasis is not on the story but on the emotional flow; what the female director does is not to narrate what a character experiences but to reveal how they experience it. In *The Blue Wave*, for instance, the directors try to explore how Deniz and her friends experience and perceive the daily things, how they feel, rather than trying to accurately record the incidents. It is their frustration, disappointment, and excitement that the directors are concerned with, not their actions. In this sense, the film is interested in the "vertical investigation of a situation" rather than simply displaying what is happening.

How these emotions are depicted projects the political characteristic of the aesthetics used in Women's New Cinema. Unlike the "heteronormative" narratives where the couples complete each other, the female characters of *The Blue Wave* do not complete each other but nor do they exclude each other—they include each other. They make mistakes but they do not judge or blame each other; they share their emotions and ideas. The directors do not construct excessive emotions via the use of style but provide experiences of emotions lived through a daily routine. The experiences of the characters do not lead to over-emotional or traumatic consequences. On this topic, Dadak and Kayan say:

> And two women are making movies, what do they have to say? This is not just about Turkey. In many parts of the world there is a tradition of limiting stories, issues, films. Unfortunately, as Merve [Kayan] said, this is the tradition of this country. Big brothers tell important stories. An important story must necessarily be painful, and great things must happen. However, pain and distress are experienced by permeating people through daily life. This is probably what we will be dealing with in cinema from now on: not the blessing of pain, but how emotions can arise in other situations. (2014)

Dadak and Kayan refer to the rules and codes of classical narratives with traditional storytelling. As conceptualized by film theorists David Bordwell, Janet Staiger, and Kristin Thompson (1985), the classical Hollywood style of film storytelling has distinctive conventions. Each plotline follows a structure often organized around a main protagonist who has a tangible goal. Conventional narrative films reinforce the romantic union as a central value. Whether blessing or cursing emotions, they associate certain lifestyles with certain feelings. By associating a certain kind of being with pain or happiness, they formulate a world in which they determine which life choice leads to which feeling.[3] Instructing the spectator on how to feel and what to think, the classical narratives are authoritative. As Christine Gledhill also mentions:

> The subject of mainstream narrative is the patriarchal, bourgeois individual: that unified, centred point from which the world is organized and given meaning. Narrative organization hierarchizes the different aesthetic and ideological discourses which intersect in the processes of the text, to produce a unifying, authoritative voice or viewpoint. This is the position constructed outside the processes of contradiction, difference and meaning production which the spectator must occupy in order to participate in the pleasures and meaning of the text. (1999, 167)

In contrast, the distribution of emotions into the happenings of daily life, not emphasizing pain or happiness, and refusing to satisfy the spectator by closing the film with a clear ending, adds a feminist and political emphasis to the films belonging to Women's New Cinema. *The Blue Wave,* for instance, does not focus on emotions, therefore it "fails" to tell us how to feel. Not dictating how to feel, the film provides us with an anti-oppressive way of seeing. Spoiling the visual pleasure[4] by leaving the scenes "incomplete," this film allocates space for the spectator to produce her own meaning. In the narrative, the viewer is not provided with a reason for constant gas and electric cuts, not everyone's story is told (such as the repairwoman), and not every detail is shared with the viewers (e.g., the camera does not show Gül's tattoo). It is in this sense that the aesthetics of Women's New Cinema are anti-authoritative. Other movies such as *Present Tense*, *Motherland*, *Zephyr*, and *Something Useful* also have narratives that are anti-oppressive. Their scenes are not sealed with a certain kind of meaning or feeling but open to different understandings and implications.

Open images are also "a feature of film endings, closing scenes which try not to close down a narrative but rather open it out to the viewer's consideration, to 'live on' after the film itself has finished" (Chaudhuri and Finn 2003, 52). The mainstream classical narratives complete themselves, close themselves to other meanings. Relating the spectator to the fictional characters through identification, they draw the spectator into the film "so that when the questions posed by the narrative are resolved by its closure, the spectator is also 'closed', completed or satisfied" (Kuhn 1994, 152). As observed by Barbara Creed, however, historically, female directors prefer to leave their films open; in other words, they refuse to close their narratives, "perhaps because they adopt an oppositional stance in relation not only to their subject matter but also in relation to conventional cinematic practices" (Blonski, Creed and Freiberg 1987, 309). Where things are congealed is the space of the finite, while leaving the film open allocates a space for obscurity which creates a space for the infinite. From this perspective, I evaluate the open endings of the films belonging to Women's New Cinema as quite feminist. In *The Blue* Wave, for example, there is not one single event that needs to be resolved so that the film can finalize itself; it ends without closing itself. After bidding farewell to Kaya, who is moving to another city to study at the university, Deniz and her friends leave the bus at the traffic lights and walk away slowly and aimlessly, exiting out of the static frame. Instead of feeling like closure, this last sequence implies a dedramatic everyday happening. Because the plot events remain unresolved, the audience carries the film with them out of the theatre and continues feeling and thinking about the film and the lives of Deniz and her friends. In this sense, the film permeates into life, which allows it to intervene with the flow of life. It also creates a space for the contribution of the audience, inviting the audience into the creative process.

Figure 4.1 The end of *Present Tense*; when the cups get cleaned, what happens to the fortunes?

Present Tense (Figure 4.1), *Lifelong*, *Dust Cloth*, *Zephyr*, *Motherland* and *Something Useful* are other films from Women's New Cinema that conclude by leaving the end open. The endings of these films open themselves to new meanings and interpretations. In this sense, they create a meaningful story by collaborating with their audience.[5] The narratives of these films do not reach a conclusion or solution—just like the differences and heterogeneity within women.[6]

The inconclusive films of Women's New Cinema also have another sense of temporality which corresponds to the notion of Julia Kristeva's "women's time." In her influential essay "Women's Time," Kristeva talks about two temporal dimensions: "the time of linear history" that is concerned with the "problems of the *production* of material goods (i.e., the domain of the economy and of the human relationships it implies, politics, and so on)" and "the time of another history thus another time" that concerns the "*reproduction*, survival of the species, life and death, the body, sex, and symbol" (1981, 14; original emphasis). I associate the first temporality with the conventional narrative films that flow in a linear manner; it is about a beginning and an end. Women's time, however, gives a more cyclic and repetitive rhythm to time and I associate this latter temporality with *The Blue Wave* and several other films of Women's New Cinema such as *Hayaletler/Ghosts*, a film made by Azra Deniz Okyay in 2020. In *The Blue Wave,* we watch Deniz repeatedly trying to get a painting repaired; despite her frustration, she continues going to the repairwoman's store. Her mood swings permeate the rhythm of the city; we watch repeated gas, electricity, and water cuts. Besides the repetitive rhythm of the narrative, the repetitive rhythm of the scenes creates a cyclic temporality. There are many scenes that create tension but fail to create a conflict and resolve it. It feels like the audience is carried to the edge of a cliff each time but is prevented from jumping down. This act of rising and "failing" to reach the climax and catharsis adds to the repetitive sense of temporality. Refusing a linear flow and cathartic resolutions, *The Blue Wave* adopts the aesthetics of feminist narratives. Not choosing a heroic and cathartic narrative but a feminist one is a political act: it projects the feminist statement of the directors and the editor Çiçek Kahraman, who openly identify themselves as feminists (İnceoğlu 2015, 88).

Understated Acting and Dedramatization

To evaluate the strategies practiced by the female directors of Women's New Cinema and the politics and logic behind them, I continue to analyze the aesthetic choices of Dadak and Kayan through the concept "open image." One of the most significant characteristics of "open image" is its "involving understated acting and dedramatization" (Chaudhuri and Finn 2003, 41). We see the same characteristics in *The Blue Wave*'s dramatic structure. There are many scenes in which we watch the tension rise but the directors "fail" our expectations of a conflict. As stated by İnceoğlu, these young people smoke, drink, and flirt with each other but nothing unpleasant occurs; the drunk boys do not harass the girls, the girls do not fight with each other to attract the boys' attention, they do not race to become more popular than each other (2015, 91). There are no tense or violent scenes in which women are victimized. Even the unequal relationship between Deniz and her teacher Fırat is presented as equal, as Deniz is depicted as a powerful young woman. The directors chose to tell their story by adopting a different kind of dramatic structure: a dedramatic one. On this choice, they say:

> When you look at it, there was such a thing as the avant-garde back in 1900. The emergence of a cinematic language, which has become obsessed with drama, coincides with later. On the other hand, what is this love of conflict . . . In fact, it's about what/who is dominating. There is this a particular way of making a movie and some people care more about it. This is not just something unique here, it happens in every country. These people try to hold a door, and when someone else comes through that door, they try to kick them. I don't think we're doing anything very interesting in that sense. I'm even surprised when I look at it; in 2014, there is still a debate about whether there is a dramatic conflict or not. It is not like there is no dramatic conflict in this movie; there is but it is a different form of conflict. (Dadak and Kayan 2014)

A film with a distinct dramatic structure is favored as a convention of filmmaking more than films with a dedramatic structure. That is why Dadak and Kayan have been harshly criticized by male critics. The critics describe the film as "a faded story with no conflict in it," "completely dead to character and human relations," having "no serious incidents," and "a smiling movie" (quoted in İnceoğlu 2015, 89). These quotes reveal that critics are used to the overdramatic, conventional heteronormative narratives made by the "big brothers," that is, the male auteurs of the New Cinema of Turkey. They also show how the traditions are protected and sustained by the patriarchal film industry. The directors had a choice about whether to comply with the hegemonic discourse. Bravely, they chose an alternative structure that is "far from heroic. Far from the masculine promises of pleasure that always miss the pleasure itself. Intertwined with the everyday, worldly, and finite" (U. T. Arslan 2021).

The hegemonic discourse has close ties not only with patriarchy but also with capitalism. As named by Vietnamese American author Ocean Voung, this dramatic structure is a "capitalistic promise" or a "phallic manipulation" that sells release (Vuong 2020). By building a narrative based on conflict, the audience is emotionally manipulated toward a climax and then feels free. "We buy false freedom," says Vuong and asks, "How do we find a way to talk about life that is actually not free?" (Vuong 2020) How can the dedramatic aesthetics help us to produce such a narrative that captures the complexity of things?

The dedramatic approach has the ability to depict things in their complexity as it uses non-dualistic narrative logic. Non-duality, as defined by Vuong (2020), is an ancient method used by Eastern narratology (see Kishōtenketsu). While the ancient Greek, Roman, and modern Western literature build the narrative in dualistic terms in alignment with Aristotelian logic which states that A is A, A is not non-A, and A cannot be A and non-A, the dedramatic structure uses the paradoxical logic of East which says "That which is one is one. That which is not-one, is also one" (see Chuang-tzu as quoted in Fromm 1956, 73–4 and Sufi metaphysics, *Waḥdat al-wujūd*). Rather than building a climax by using a binary gaze such as good versus bad, villain versus victim, and men versus nature, the dedramatic structure creates tension by lying images side by side and uses "proximity" to build the narrative (Vuong 2020). "When you do not have conflict," says Vuong, "you have people who can have the opportunity to pursue their lives in their own terms" (2020).

Failing to fulfil the expectation of a conflict between female characters, *The Blue Wave* adapts the logic of dedramatic narrative structure. This adds a political and feminist dimension to the film. By invalidating discourses such as "how women try to rule each other out for the attention of the desired man," the film reverses the narrative of conflict that is claimed to be specific to femininity and adopts an alternative discourse (İnceoğlu 2015, 89). Within this discourse, the relationship among the girls is presented as one of friendship and solidarity. *Dust Cloth*, *The Play*, *Queen Lear*, *Clair Obscur*, *Present Tense*, and *Dream Workers* are other films of Women's New Cinema that are characterized by female solidarity and friendship. Avoiding creating dramatic conflict via conflict between women, these films subvert the phallic expectations and strengthen the feminist statement of Women's New Cinema.

Last but not least, the dedramatic narrative structure affects the presentation of the female body. In *The Blue Wave*, the images of the girls are not aestheticized nor fetishized as they are in most Turkish dramatic films. The film limits what we as spectators can demand to see in people of this age. We see them make up, but it is a moment of joy shared together rather than a struggle to attract a boy's attention. In another scene, Gül unbuttons her trousers to show her tattoo to her friends but she turns her back on the camera/us and her friends cover her. Not finalizing itself with a definite image, this sequence reads as an open image. In her detailed analysis, Didem Nur Güngören comments on this scene as follows:

> A border is drawn, and even we, who have witnessed their world from the inside, cannot cross it. As a moral proposition, our knowing and understanding of certain things is not enough for these people's lives/bodies to be revealed to us "adults," we cannot violate this limit, we cannot demand its violation even in the name of giving love. There is a distance between us and these people who continue their lives by growing, which is invisible to them but fixed for us. And not to cross that distance by making it invisible for them so that they will not be harmed, not to demand that it be exceeded, as a responsibility far beyond the "duties and responsibilities" imposed on young people, is included in the domain of adults. (2014)

The Blue Wave does not close the scene by presenting the girls as objects of a voyeuristic gaze as it does not present the girls for us but puts a boundary between the girls and us. By leaving the image open, the directors own the responsibility of showing: how do we see, what is made invisible, and what do we see? As Sharpe reminds us, "Visuality is not simply looking. It is a regime of seeing and being" (2023, 123). Seeing here is not simply a sense but it is immanent to power relations with its political and social value.

The Unsympathetic Characters

To understand the political aesthetics of New Women's Cinema, it is necessary to also consider the role of unsympathetic characters in these films. Chaudhuri and Finn compare classical Hollywood narratives with New Iranian Cinema by examining the latter's unsympathetic character type. "In an added self-reflexive ambiguity many of these central characters [of New Iranian Cinema] are film directors: seemingly insensitive and aloof manipulators of their casts" (Chaudhuri and Finn 2003, 51). In contrast, conventional narrative films present the protagonist as a sympathetic character despite his foibles. As a result, we mostly identify with his actions and emotions; we affirm and confirm his actions and evaluate the other characters according to his moral codes (2003, 51). Unlike conventional narrative films, the presence of unsympathetic characters is central to Women's New Cinema. The contemporary female directors of Women's New Cinema are not concerned with creating character empathy to make the viewer easily identify with the protagonist. I now evaluate the features and functions of this character within the films.

The directors of *The Blue Wave* say, "Loving our main character is not that easy. She has a strange arrogance. She seems like she doesn't care about being a part of the group, but she obviously does . . . We also found it important to create a character that could not be related to at first glance" (Dadak and Kayan 2014). Similarly, in *Until I Lose My Breath*, Emine Emel Balcı tells the story of Serap, an anti-heroine who the director does little to make likable. In *Zephyr*, Belma Baş tells the story of Zefir, who kills her mother because her mother wants to leave and live without her. In this story, not only the child but also the mother are presented as characters that the audience cannot identify with easily. In *Dust Cloth*, one of the main protagonists, Nesrin, leaves her home and child while in *Clair Obscur*, Elmas kills her husband and Şehnaz cheats on her husband. In *What Remains*, we can neither identify with Sevda, a housewife who is being cheated on by her husband, Cezmi, nor with Zuhal, with whom Cemil cheats on her wife.

The female characters of Women's New Cinema—Deniz, Zefir, Elmas, Nesrin, Şehnaz, Zuhal, Sevda—are not presented as heroines or villains. They are merely depicted within their ordinary lives. For instance, in *The Blue Wave*, although Deniz is the protagonist, she is not the heroine. It is not only Deniz who is significant in the narrative but also her girlfriends. The directors present the everyday life of a few young middle-class women living in the countryside by rejecting the "heroic" existence of the protagonists and the masculine language based on the unfolding of a heroic story throughout the film. In this sense, the film presents a narrative that we are not very accustomed to. It activates an empowering political language that does not rise in tension; it is not about victims or heroes but about young women discovering their own individuality (Inceoglu 2015, 89).

As the characters of Women's New Cinema are not heroines with whom we can immediately feel sympathy, it is not easy to identify with them. According to Chaudhuri and Finn, "The failure of identification with characters snaps the sensory-motor chain, and liberates the senses we become more receptive to other aspects of the film. In particular, it facilitates connections with virtual images which will return in the viewer's memory" (2003, 51). Agreeing with them, I argue that the failure of identification also creates a space between the film and the viewer; the protagonist and the viewer do not become one but stay as themselves. This distance is a space where the audience can meditate on the film's meaning and reflect upon its narrative. Not using heroines nor the impact of identification, I argue that these films communicate with their audience in another language which is non-hierarchical. I understand this non-hierarchical language as horizontal aesthetics. While the capitalistic promise and the phallic manipulation necessitate hierarchical narratives, what the dedramatized structure of Women's New Cinema offers is non-hierarchical horizontal aesthetics. This approach is based on "foundation," a wide space where the hierarchies are flattened (Vuong 2022). "The wider one goes the more space one sees," says Vuong (2022), "but the higher one looks, the less there is to see." This approach allows the narratives of Women's New Cinema to capture the importance of many things, hold space for more human experience, and provide the audience with endless possibilities for interpretation.

Women's New Cinema includes many female stories that refuse heroic narratives and adopt horizontal aesthetics. In *Present Tense*, Fazi's story as significant as Mina's. Similarly, *Clair Obscur* and *Dust Cloth* have two female protagonists. Pelin Esmer's *The Play* and *Queen Lear* tell the stories of several women. In *A Fatal Dress: Polygamy*, Mizgin Müjde Arslan narrates the stories of Kurdish women. In these films, no one woman's story dominates; instead, the directors offer multiple perspectives. Each point of view is equally unique and valuable. There is no hierarchy between the characters. This non-hierarchical language and non-heroic narratives strengthen the political and feminist discourse of Women's New Cinema.

Conclusion: Dare to Stumble

In this chapter, I evaluated the various aesthetic tactics adopted by the female directors of Women's New Cinema by discussing the film *The Blue Wave*. The usage of the dull, banal happenings of the everyday, telling the story of the ordinary, the dedramatized narrative structure, the lack of fetishization of the female body, unsympathetic characters, failure of identification, and using a cyclic time and cyclic rhythm are the aesthetic tactics adapted by *The Blue Wave* and several other films of Women's New Cinema such as *Present Tense, Motherland, Zephyr, Lifelong, Dust Cloth, Clair Obscur*, and *Something Useful*. These qualities can also be found in other cinema movements such as Third Cinema, the Iranian New Wave, slow cinema and Italian neorealism. However, the contemporary female filmmakers of Women's New Cinema use these aesthetic strategies to subvert, deconstruct, or destabilize hegemonic, sexist language, allowing us to see the world in a new way or gaze through which we can see her ways of living. The directors of Women's New Cinema make anti-oppressive, feminist, and ethical filmmaking models visible in the national cinematic scene. That is why I describe their aesthetics as political, an umbrella term including all the features of this aesthetic approach.

Although the directors of Women's New Cinema have not dismantled the master's house yet, they dare to try. At this point, I would like to echo the words of one of the directors of Women's New Cinema, Çiğdem Vitrinel, who explains how she struggles against the language constructed by the patriarchy. She says:

> Latife Tekin righteously says: "Just like the poor, women are also without history. Women need to reject history because men wrote it." When a woman sets out to create herself, she must reject all that language, discourse, and history of art and politics that centered only on white, middle-class, heterosexual men. But how, by what means, and substituting with what? That was my main issue. But it is not a problem that we can solve within a few books or a movie at once. Because the ways of thinking that naturalize and legitimize this order have of course also polluted our minds. So, all I could do was dare to stumble, get lost, allow the slip of my tongue. I released myself, Sevda and Zuhal [the female characters of *What Remains*] with all our confusion and inconsistency. (Aytaç and Göl 2012)

Women's New Cinema is about insisting: to dare, to dare to get lost, to enter new, unknown paths. It is the tools we invent through daring to stumble that will dismantle the master's house.

Notes

1. I named this chapter after Audre Lorde's influential essay "The Master's Tools Will Never Dismantle the Master's House" (1984b).
2. I would like to thank Professor Sanem Yazıcıoğlu for the insightful conversation that sharpened my understanding of women's political aesthetics.
3. Here we can think of "the figure of happy housewife," "the myth of happy slave," or "the sentimentalization of heterosexuality as a domestic bliss" (Ahmed 2010, 2). These examples show us how happiness is used to describe social norms (2010, 2). See *The Promise of Happiness* (Ahmed 2010) for an extended reading of the relationship of certain feelings and certain kind of beings.
4. See "Visual Pleasure and Narrative Cinema" (Mulvey [1975] 1999) for an extended description of how the patriarchal codes of classical narratives produce pleasure for the male gaze.
5. Chapter 5 discusses this collaboration in detail.
6. Here, I am using the perspective of Umut Tümay Arslan (2022c).

Chapter 5

"Because of Her, We Can": Subjectivity and Collectivity in Women's New Cinema[1]

In 2005, Pelin Esmer, one of the most influential directors of Women's New Cinema, made a documentary film, *The Play*, that narrated the journey of nine village women from Arslanköy (a mountain village in southern Turkey). The film documents them preparing a theatre play based on their real lives to perform for their own community. I saw the film in the summer of 2018 when I was doing extensive research to prepare my PhD proposal. I remember my excitement at witnessing the will of the participants and the sense that I had found something here: the new perspectives contemporary women's cinema can offer. Inspired by my "discovery," I designed a doctoral project, where my story entangles with the stories of this women's theatre group and the story of female directors. In 2019, Pelin Esmer made another documentary, *Queen Lear*, in which the same village women not only present a new theatre play to the neighboring villages but they also screen the film *The Play*. In 2020, during the filming of my documentary, Pelin Esmer told the story of *Queen Lear* as follows:

> They [Arslanköy village women's theatre group] screened the movie *The Play* and they were also watching it for the first time after 14 years. They made the other villagers watch the film, the audience was the neighbours that they drank tea with, milked cows together . . . They were showing themselves as examples: "We're just like you, there's no difference between us. I milk cows, I have herded goats for 17 years and you do the same. If I can do it, you can do it too." (Esmer quoted in Fontini 2020; personal communication)

What I like the most in this story is how all parties transformed into each other. As a spectator of *The Play*, I interviewed Pelin Esmer and the Arslanköy village women's theatre group; they also became participants in my documentary film *Dream Workers*; while the Arslanköy village women's theatre group became the spectator of their own performance during the shootings of *Queen Lear* . . . All parties are active because of the subject position we occupy in each role. As a way of recognizing and honoring the works of these village women, I consider the subjectivity and collectivity invoked by the sentence, "If I can do it, you can do it too" throughout this chapter, using it as a means of thinking through the strategies and modes of spectatorship locatable in Women's New Cinema.

This chapter analyzes Pelin Esmer's subjectivity through her documentary *The Play*. Understanding subjectivity as the directorial persona, I examine how Esmer constructs her narrative, how she collaborates with the subjects of the documentary, and how her directorial subjectivity influences the recording of their experience. For this, I think through the new documentary terminology developed by Jill Godmilow such as "pornography of reality," "pedigree of the real," and "imperialism of the real" (2022, 31). However, instead of naming non-conventional documentaries as "postrealist," as does Godmilow (2022, 31), I aim to coin a new term, "experiential,"[2] to describe Esmer's filmmaking mode. In the second part of my discussion, I explore the subjectivity of the audience. Instead of understanding spectatorship as a construction (see Smelik 1998, 1), I aim to think of the audience as the subject—that is, understanding the viewing experience as something active, as a "negotiation" (see Gledhill 1999), rather than evaluating that experience as being in a passive state. Thinking through the ideas of Jacques Rancière (2009) on "emancipated audience," I will discuss the subjectivity of the female audience, which is to consider the audience as a more equal party in the process of creating meaning. This perspective not only brings about the emancipation of the audience but also subverts rigid boundaries such as producer/consumer, constructing/constructed, and active/passive, and opens the doors to a non-hierarchical space that can be the place of the feminist ethics.[3] Through these discussions, I will theorize the subjectivity and collectivity of women's filmmaking in Turkey and pose these as new aspects immanent to Women's New Cinema.

"I" as a Feminist Tactic: The Subjectivity of the Director

Experiential Filmmaking: Who the Director Chooses to Be

Released in 2005, *The Play* is the second documentary made by Pelin Esmer. At the center of its narrative are nine women from the Arslanköy village: Ümmüye, Ümmü, Behiye, Fatma K, Saniye, Fatma F, Cennet, Nesime, and Zeynep. These women work in the fields, on construction sites, and at home. They herd goats, milk cows, look after children, cook, and clean their houses (Figure 5.1).

One day, they decide to write a script based on their own life stories and perform it for the village. They start gathering in the high school of the village and with the help of the schoolteacher, Mr Hüseyin, they write a play which contains the details of their life stories: not receiving a proper education, being forced

Figure 5.1 Esmer's camera recording women cooking food. A still from *The Play*.

to marry, experiencing domestic violence—details they have never confronted before. Together they create an entertaining and sometimes dramatic play and start rehearsing it under the curious glances of the village people. *The Play* is a documentary reflecting this creative process.

Upon reading the news about the theatre group, Esmer decided to visit the village women. When she arrived at the village, she did not start filming immediately but spent a couple of days with them; they sewed her an outfit typically worn by village women and Esmer wore it during the filmmaking process (Figure 5.2). She says "the outfit became a symbol of our seeing each other equal" (Esmer quoted in Kırel 2009, 130).

Before arriving at the village, Esmer was feeling "very curious as a human being and want[ed] to get to know them" (Esmer quoted in Kırel 2009, 131). She was motivated to make the documentary because she wanted to be "a guest in their world" (Esmer quoted in Fontini 2020; personal communication). Esmer did not exist only as a filmmaker; she was a guest, visiting them to get to know them. Esmer made *The Play* so she could "experience their experience together with them [Arslanköy village women]" and "transform into someone new" (Esmer quoted in Fontini 2020; personal communication). In this sense,

Figure 5.2 Pelin Esmer, wearing the same outfit as village women, films their journey. A still from the backstage of *The Play*.

her filmmaking is not only a way of producing but also a livingness. Esmer is not interested in looking at the subjects to show them to an audience, but she is concerned with living through the process while recording it.

It is this approach that turns Esmer's filmmaking into an "experiential" one. With experiential filmmaking, I refer to an affective filmmaking model in which the director experiences the experience of making a film. There is a reason why experiential filmmaking repeats the word "experience" two times. When I speak of experiential filmmaking, I am not only speaking about the way the filmmaker makes her film (her methodology of making a film, her filmmaking experience) but also the way she prefers to be (her methodology of living life, her life experience). "The questions of how another kind of recording, another kind of seeing/hearing happens" always "bring about the necessity of considering a perspective that is not independent of the observer" (Arslan 2022). That is why in this section, I aim to explore the experiential mode as a way of experiencing life, and in the next section, I will analyze it as a filmmaking model.

Inspired by Esmer, I understand experiential mode as a creative being and a *felt* experience that is sustained by the "erotic" (see Lorde [1984] 2007), "wonder" (see McKittrick 2021, 6), and coincidence. Esmer was open to unmet possibility and surprise—that is how the story of Arslanköy village women found her. Upon reading the story in a newspaper, Esmer hit the road because she had the desire to know. She "dropped everything just to have that adventure, to experience it" (Esmer quoted in Fontini 2020; personal communication). "How many times can you get to see," says Esmer, "that in a village where there is no road, no water supply, or visitor there is a theatre company?" (Esmer quoted in Fontini 2020; personal communication). It is this "attentive curiosity" (McKittrick 2021, 5) that turns the process into an erotic one.

In her inspiring essay "Uses of the Erotic," Audre Lorde says erotic is "not a question only of what we do; it is a question of how acutely and fully we can feel in the doing ([1984] 2007, 54). Esmer's motivation to go to Arslanköy was not to document the theatre play but to "experience the excitement" of village women's writing and acting in a theatre play (Esmer quoted in Fontini 2020; personal communication). Esmer was sharing the joy of the village women which is why she was feeling she was a part of their experience (Esmer quoted in Fontini 2020; personal communication). It is Esmer's "capacity for joy" through which the erotic functions. The willingness to share joy, says Lorde "forms a bridge between the sharers which can be the basis for understanding much of what is not shared between them, and lessens the threat of their difference" ([1984] 2007, 56). The bridge of joy or the conviviality formed between Esmer and the village women enables her to witness and capture the truth—not the truth about the village women but a truth that comes out of them.

Experiential mode as a creative livingness understands life in its ancient way, "as a situation to be experienced and interacted with" rather than "as a problem to be solved" (Lorde 1984a, 37). It is a way of celebrating; not white, not right, not predetermined:

> When we view living, in the european [sic] mode, only as a problem to be solved, we then rely solely upon our ideas to make us free, for these were what the white fathers told us were precious. But as we become more in touch with our own ancient, black, non-european [sic] view of living as a situation to be experienced and interacted with, we learn more and more to cherish our feelings, and to respect those hidden sources of our power from where true knowledge and therefore lasting action comes. (1984a, 37)

Esmer's documentary is a "revelation and distillation of experience" which is a direct result of her viewing living and filmmaking as a practice "to be experienced and interacted with" (1984a, 37). The source of true knowledge and access to the real is this experience, not the look that lacks insight.

Lorde understands pornography as the opposite of the erotic source and defines it as "sensation without feeling" ([1984] 2007, 54). Pornography, as a "suppression of true feeling," ([1984] 2007, 54) is a capitalistic force that is interested in how fast we consume life. In her groundbreaking work *Kill the Documentary*, Godmilow (2022) coins a similar terminology to define particular film forms. Introducing Godmilow's terminology in the foreword of her book, Bill Nichols says:

> Dominant conventions of realism move toward pornography in which the people in a documentary, like the women in a Playboy centerfold, are reduced to their usefulness to the filmmaker and his vision (these works are predominantly by men). This, she [Godmilow] argues, is pornography. A pornography of the real . . . It is empathy for the individual subject not understanding of the systemic issue shrouded beneath a feel-good liberalism. (Nicols quoted in Godmilow 2022, xii–xiii)

Documentary as "pornography of reality" argues that conventional documentaries are pornographic if they depict persons or things to be circulated, commodified, and consumed without regard to their subject status (Godmilow 2022, 13). These documentaries present accuracies and truths for viewers to care about momentarily so that the problem is no longer ours. "We" watch "them" so as to become good, knowledgeable citizens (2022, 15). But Esmer's film wants to awaken us from this hegemonic, neoliberal way of thinking. I evaluate *The Play* as an experiential documentary because Esmer does not produce (victimized) Eastern femininity for our consumption. She refuses to create binaries such as us/them, gender liberated/enslaved, developed/underdeveloped, civilized/primitive, therefore resisting "the allure of realism of documentary (as pornography)" (Godmilow 2022, 3). This was not a tactic adopted by the director but an ethical statement that understands the importance of care to the participants, in this instance the village women.

Experiential Filmmaking: How the Director Chooses to Make her Film

Experiential mode as a documentary-making methodology is sustained by care; it is being conscious about how caring contributes to creating. What are the acts and accounts of care here? How does a caring look see and a caring ear hear? In her influential book *Ordinary Notes*, Christina Sharpe defines care as a "refusal of an unbearable life," a "total rejection of a dead future" (2023, 333). How can such a life description be a filmmaking prescription?

To Sharpe, care "is often mobilized to enact violence, not assuage it" (2023, 333). Her understanding makes me think of how certain films turn violence into a spectacle and/or reproduce violence by denying the possibility of "imagining otherwise" (Sharpe 2016). These filmmakers tell us "status-quo stories" which are "worldviews that normalize and naturalize the existing social system, values, and standards so entirely that they prevent us from imagining the possibility of change" (Keating 2013, 35). They claim to provide us with a "realist" perspective but "do little to get us thinking about their assumptions" (Nichols quoted in Godmilow 2022, xv). "Instead, they simply display their presumption to hold before us a truth about the world" (2022, xv). As "vision is always a question of the power to see—and perhaps of the violence implicit in our visualizing practices," we need to ask ourselves this urgent question: "With whose blood have our eyes been crafted?" (Haraway 1988, 585). Godmilow provides us with an answer:

> It has commonly been white, first-world filmmakers who go in search of people who are in trouble, need help of some kind, or who are ethnographically interesting. In this process, the personhood of the people being filmed is often lost, and the values and aesthetics of their culture are compressed, but rarely expressed, by the filmmaking itself. (2022, 101)

In her "Open Letter to Mary Daly," Lorde asks Daly a question. It is not a rhetorical question: "Have you read my work, and the work of other Black women, for what it could give you . . . Did you ever read my words, or did you merely finger through them for quotations?" ([1984] 2007, 68–9). This is how the first world often connects with the "other." Adapting Lorde's questioning to Godmilow's description above, I can possibly say that majorly white, Western documentary makers search for quotations in people's lives that can legitimize their worldview; their view on the "other." It is a non-caring gaze processing the "naturalistic performances" of "informants" into "cultural identities" to sell in Western festival circles; this is how filmmaking is turned into a colonizing practice. Instead of playing these Westerncentric games, we need a pedagogy of looking. In this sense, I find the experiential mode as an antidote.

Experiential filmmaker has the preparedness or maturity to "notice" or "observe with care" (Sharpe 2023, 349). It means practicing relational ethics (to bridge) between the filmmaker, participants, and audience. During our interview, Esmer defined her documentary-making process as an "experience of bringing our eye levels closer" (Esmer quoted in Fontini 2020; personal communication). Her filmmaking description is a bridging definition. "To bridge," says Keating, "is to attempt community, and for that we must risk being open to personal, political, and spiritual intimacy, to risk being wounded" (2013, 42). The "our" in Esmer's sentence is to "attempt community," it indicates an egalitarian and intimate connection not only between the director and the village women but also between the director and the spectator.

In *Sister Outsider*, Audre Lorde asks another striking question: "Why don't we meet each other's eyes? Do we expect betrayal in each other's gaze, or recognition?" ([1984] 2007, 155). In *The Play*, Esmer is not interested in observing and objectifying the village women with a voyeuristic gaze. Her aim is not "to entertain its audience; to produce fascination with its materials; to achieve closure; to satisfy, and to assure the audience of informed and moral citizenship" as conventional documentary does (Godmilow 2022, 2–3). That is how she is able to meet the participants' eyes and find recognition there. She invites the spectator to meet their gaze instead of consuming village women as images without regard to their status as subjects. Promoting a more equal mode of looking and engagement, Esmer's mode of address here is political and non-hierarchical, which I call experiential.

Although they share the same verb, observing with care is quite different from the observational documentary-making mode. In observational mode, the filmmaker's presence is minimized to "elicit highly naturalistic performances" and "the vivid impression of people 'being themselves'" (Nichols 1991, xvi, 13). Observational documentaries are about recording the observations of the filmmaker or observing someone else's life (1991, 39). In *The Play*, Esmer chooses not to intervene in the flow of the events, which is why her mode of documentary-making can be identified as "observational." But this is exactly what Esmer does not do; in her own words, she avoids the feeling of "I came from the city, I am observing you" (Esmer quoted in Kırel 2009, 131).

I understand Esmer's choice of not intervening in the flow of the events as an ethical statement: it is about leaving a gap, a boundary perhaps, between the participants and the director. The gap left by Esmer is filled by the village women. In this sense, the director does not make a film "about" the village women but as I will explore further in the next section, they "co-create" the film together. Trinh T. Minh-ha explains the gap between the participants and the filmmaker with the notion of "speaking nearby":

> When you decide to speak nearby, rather than speak about, the first thing you need to do is to acknowledge the possible gap between you and those who populate your film: in other words, to leave the space of representation open so that, although you're very close to your subject, you're also committed to not speaking on their behalf, in their place or on top of them. You can only speak nearby, in proximity, which requires that you deliberately suspend meaning, preventing it from merely closing and hence leaving a gap in the formation process. This allows the other person to come in and fill that space as they wish. Such an approach gives freedom to both sides and this may account for it being taken up by filmmakers who recognize in it a strong

> ethical stance. By not trying to assume a position of authority in relation to the other, you are actually freeing yourself from the endless criteria generated with such an all-knowing claim and its hierarchies in knowledge. (Minh-ha quoted in Bolsom 2018)

When we "speak about" our participants, we "close off people, places, and events . . . We close off avenues of communication and vision so that individual and communal trust, responsibility, loving, and knowing are impossible" (Canaan 1981, 236). When we "speak nearby," on the other hand, we create a space for the community to make itself possible. This is what I call co-creating together. In a cinematic landscape in which mostly men and white Turkish women produce, making a film together with village women is a subversion of the hegemonic mode of filmmaking. This is another definition of experiential documentary: not to make a film about the participants but to make a film together with them.

Creating a gap so the participants speak themselves requires the director to remain silent and listen with serious intent. As Mitsuye Yamada says, "one of the most insidious ways of keeping women and minorities powerless is to . . . let them speak freely and not listen to them with serious intent" (1981, 40). According to Keating, it is the result of "binary-oppositional politics" (2013, 54). In such situations, we can be:

> very quick to judge each other—often in negative, extremely harsh terms. Yet these judgments are driven by overly simplistic status-quo thinking based on stereotypes that invite superficial judgments: We look at a person, label her, and categorize her based on these labels. We assume that we fully know her position, motivations, values, and beliefs. We know her . . . because of her appearance and the identity groups to which she seems to belong, because of her previous comments, because of her overly assertive tone, or because of other such external signs. How can we be so confident in this knowledge? (Keating 2013, 54)

Keating's alternative to this stereotyping binary-oppositional politics is listening with "raw openness," which, to me, is another way of defining caring ears. In *The Play*, the cliches about the village women were shattered because Esmer approached them with open ears. Instead of naming, inspecting, or defining the village women, she created a space of wonder which made knowing possible.

Esmer's desire to know stems from her consciousness which knows that she does not know. It is Esmer's "intellectual humility" (Keating 2013, 55) that enables her to acknowledge her epistemological limitations. Keating says listening with "raw openness" "takes tremendous effort" and "demands vulnerability"

(2013, 52). It demands vulnerability or the risk of being wounded because it is about confronting one's own incompleteness. As Haraway reminds us, "The knowing self is partial in all its guises, never finished, whole, simply there and original; it is always constructed and stitched together imperfectly, and therefore able to join with another, to see together without claiming to be another" (Haraway 1988, 586). This brings us back to situatedness:

> Why is it necessary to think of knowledge as situated, partial, embodied? What does it mean that different bodies share different ways of seeing, feeling and hearing? What does this say about the community we call "we"? Movies are of course very helpful in understanding this. Are we positioned outside and above the narrated world, or embedded in it and its contradictions? Am I the invisible source of the world I watch, or am I in this world, so far below that I can encounter the fragility of being under the nomadic observation of a gaze, that I can encounter others due to my constant openness? (U. T. Arslan 2022c)

Acknowledging one's own position, and imperfections is a way to gain hearing ears. In this way, the director can manage not to position herself outside or above the narrated world. Caring ears also mean not to position the other somewhere below. This is what Esmer alluded to when describing the experience of bringing our eye levels closer. It is about being able to respond with one's own vulnerability once encountering the other's openness.

Being open to hearing also "requires a willingness to be altered by the words spoken" (Keating 2013, 52). It is about being ready to be changed by what one hears. Because to understand:

> is to transform, to become something else . . . To understand someone, something, an animal, a plant, or a piece of rock is to become her, a piece of her grows into you bodily, in your blood, in your nerves . . . To understand is to go towards a place that is neither you nor her anymore, it is to turn into something other than what you even understand. (Geçgin 2018, 166)

Esmer's motivation to go to Arslanköy was to "transform into someone new" (Esmer quoted in Fontini 2020; personal communication). Experiential mode, in this sense, is about daring to knock on the door opening to the as-yet-unknowns about the other and one's own.

I understand the particularities of experiential mode—erotic, wonder, coincidentiality, observing with care, speaking nearby, and listening with raw openness—as the major principles that build Esmer's subjectivity leading her to produce *The Play*. Other films (fiction and documentary) belonging to

Women's New Cinema, such as *Queen Lear*, *Waiting for the Clouds*, *Journey to the Sun*, *I Flew You Stayed*, *Present Tense*, *Clair Obscur*, *Dream Workers*, and *Dust Cloth*, can be identified as experiential as they manage to make the invisible visible by dismantling stereotypes. Producing narratives in which it is possible to imagine otherwise, they refuse an unbearable life and reject a dead future.

"We" as a Feminist Tactic: The Collectivity of Filmmaking Practice

Collaboration is a creative methodology to produce experiential documentaries. Esmer produced an experiential documentary not only because of her subjective directorial choices but also because she collaborated with the Arslanköy village women. She was not driven by a desire to investigate these "interesting" characters; they are not objects of an investigation. Owning agency and will, these women participated in the process of making meaning and the audience ends up watching a story they co-created together. I evaluate this as an act of solidarity between the filmmaker and the characters. In a similar manner, the women within *The Play* co-create the play together. In the school in which they gather, each woman tells their unique life story and the script is written based on these real-life stories. Each story is unique at the same time they are similar: the patriarchal rules, violence, forced marriages. The women end up performing each other's stories; they end up becoming the other. They encourage each other throughout the process as well; they help each other to perform the roles, practice together, and believe in each other. That is one of the reasons this chapter is entitled "because of her, we can." It is the power of being "I" and daring to tell one's real-life story to the entire village and the power of being "us" supporting each other to realize this dream together.

It is not a coincidence that other films of Women's New Cinema also tell stories of women acting collectively in their search for freedom. *Clair Obscur*, *Somewhere in Between*, *The Blue Wave*, *Present Tense*, and *Dust Cloth* feature female characters in subject positions always "failing" to fulfil the expectation of a conflict; they narrate women in solidarity. In *Something Useful* and *Bir Varmış Bir Yokmuş* (Başarır, 2015), no matter what, female characters do not judge each other for their decisions and do not turn their backs on each other; instead, they stand in solidarity. This contradicts the myth that "a woman is a woman's worst enemy." These female characters would like to see more of their sisters "trying out their wings above the mountains because freedom is not always an easy thing for women to find" (Le Guin 1975).

Women also stand in solidarity behind the camera. I, as an early career director of Women's New Cinema, prefer to work mainly with women friends because I want to understand "filmmaking" as "kinship making" (Black et al. 2024).

Similarly, Mizgin Müjde Arslan worked with a female camera person as she believed she could have better communication with a woman and they would understand each other better (Arslan quoted in Fontini 2020; personal communication). Working with female crew members is "as an expression of sisterhood, it suggests a viable alternative to the rigid hierarchical structures of male-dominated cinema and offers real opportunities for a dialogue about the nature of women's cinema within it" (Johnston 1973, 39). In this female space, women can work collectively to subvert the dominant discourses of power and they can experiment with different techniques to question the patriarchal gaze.

There are many more examples of this within the industry. For instance, Zeynep Dadak made *The Blue Wave* with Merve Kayan and it is the third film to be made in Turkey in a co-directorial partnership between two women. Filmist, a filmmaking collective consisting of mainly female directors, made *Bu Ne Güzel Demokrasi/What a Beautiful Democracy* (2008), which chronicles the struggle of women to enter the parliament. Similarly, Barış İçin Kadın Girişimi (Women for Women's Human Rights), a women's rights organization, made *Kadınlar Cizre ve Silopi'yi Anlatıyor/ Women Talk About Cizre and Silopi* (2015), narrating the collective struggle of Kurdish women against the state siege. In *What Remains*, *Fakat Müzeyyen Bu Derin Bir Tutku*, *Hush!* and *Peri Tozu*, the directors preferred to work with the female members of their families. In *Dust Cloth* and *Kumun Tadı/Seaburners* (Önel, 2014), the directors collaborated with female cinematographers. I also chose to work with a female cinematographer in *Dream Workers*; it created a safe environment in which I could express myself more comfortably. However, in Turkey the number of female directors and female crew members is quite low compared to the number of male directors and crew members (see Tanrıöver 2016). The film industry is still considered to be a men's club. This may be one of the reasons female directors prefer to work with women: to create in solidarity.

"Why Assimilate Listening to Passivity?": The Emancipation of the Female Audience[4]

When interviewing Esmer I asked what bothers her in life that leads her to make a film about it. She said:

> I begin each film with questions. If these questions are compelling for me and make me restless enough or provoke me enough, I set out on a journey after them. But I never begin this journey *with the concern to find or give an answer*. (Esmer quoted in Fontini 2020; emphasis mine)

What separates the audience "from both the capacity to know and the power to act" (Rancière 2009, 2) is this concern of the director to give an answer, to tell the audience what to think and how to feel. This perspective understands knowledge flowing from the director to the audience, from the one who knows to the one who is expected to learn. This is a "logic of straight, uniform transmission" (2009, 14). Taking the concept from the educational philosopher Joseph Jacotot, Rancière identifies this activity with that of the "stultifying pedagogue" (2009, 14). The first thing the pedagogue teaches the student is her inability. In this way, throughout the teaching activity, the teacher relentlessly confirms his own presumption; namely, the inequality of the intelligence of the student and the teacher. What the student must learn is what her teacher teaches her. What the audience needs to see is what the director shows her and what she should feel is the energy invoked by the director (2009, 14).

Jacotot comes with an alternative to this stultification, which he calls the intellectual emancipation which presumes the equality of intelligences. In this equal space, the student learns something that even the teacher himself does not know. A story, says Rancière, only finds its meaning upon meeting another story. Just like the artist, the spectator selects, compares and acts by interpreting. She relates what she sees to other things she sees in other scenes, in other places. She creates her own poem with the letters of the poem standing in front of her (Rancière 2009, 13). Or, as mentioned by Arslan, "The activity of spectatorship is not just about the place we watch or look at. It is in the back and forth between abandoning ourselves and sinking into ourselves" (U. T. Arslan 2022c) Thus Rancière calls the audience "active interpreters of the spectacle" presented to them (2009, 10–20).

Watching the films of contemporary directors from Turkey, I argue that Women's New Cinema imagines its audience as the "active interpreter of the spectacle." The directors are not teaching a moral truth or pushing a certain feeling within their films. The more I researched, the more statements of female filmmakers I came across that validated my observation. Like Esmer, Nezahat Gündoğan, one of the most influential documentary makers of Women's New Cinema, says:

> I intend the audience to be the subject of my films. I don't tell them the truths, explain them this and that in my films . . . I think of them as people who ask, think, question, and even find answers about this process, about the past, about the present and even about the future. I want my films to establish such a relationship with the audience. (Yalazan 2013)

That is why instead of focusing on how women's films in Turkey "construct" female audiences (see Smelik 1998, 1), I have pursued the question of how they address them. To unfold this idea further, I first need to briefly discuss the history of female spectatorship theory.

Influenced by cine-psychoanalysis and poststructuralism, the ideological analysis of the 1970s and '80s criticized the classical narrative style for generating "patriarchal spectatorship," asserting that conventional narrative films produce an authoritative voice, placing the patriarchal individual as the subject of the narrative and producing pleasure to flatter his patriarchal ego (see Mulvey [1975] 1999). Gledhill argues that "the psycho-linguistic location of the feminine in the repressed semiotic processes of signification led to the advocacy of the 'feminine' avant-garde or 'deconstructive' text as a means of countering the patriarchal mainstream" but the counter-cinema movement (see Johnston 1973) holds the potential to create "a comforting identity positioned in the sphere of 'ideologically correct'" (Gledhill 1999, 168). Influenced by the discussions of feminist psychoanalysts and social psychologists such as Luce Irigaray, Julia Kristeva, Nancy Chodorow, and Dorothy Dinnerstein, recent studies in feminist scholarship revisit the cine-psychoanalytic approaches to reevaluate classic film texts and to rethink the female spectatorship. They question the textual possibilities of "resistant" or "deconstructive" reading of classic texts (see Hall 1992) to "exploit textual contradiction to put into circulation readings that draw the text into a female/feminist orbit" while working on "textual and contextual analysis to determine conditions of gendered reading" (Gledhill 1999, 175). This way of evaluating spectatorship, named the "theory of negotiation" by Christine Gledhill, understands meaning production neither as "imposed" nor as "passively imbibed," but as arising "out of a struggle or negotiation between competing frames of reference, motivation and experience"; allowing space to the "subjectivities, identities and pleasures" (1999, 169, 173).

In the films of contemporary female filmmakers from Turkey, the meaning is negotiated too. These films offer space where the experiences of the female subjects meet the experiences of the female audience. Eser Köker, a prominent thinker of Turkey's culture, states that the female character has significant meaning for women who watch the movies, writing, "Expressions symbolized by a look, a challenge, a dress, a way of sitting within films have an important place in women's lives" (1994, 135). The audience comes to the theatre bringing her own experience. Watching a female character on screen having a similar or entirely different experience, she becomes able to compare experiences and produce her own meaning. Women's New Cinema addresses a female audience "not by directly depicting an experience that she feels like she belongs to, but on the contrary, by opening a place that she does not already know but can call 'me' when encountering this film" (U. T. Arslan 2022c). Not dictating a moral truth, imposing how to feel, or offering an experience that the audience feels like they belong to, the female stories of women's cinema create a space where the female audience can create a meaning that might not even be thought of by the female director. In this way, Women's New Cinema does not construct its audience but communicates with it through female images and experiences. This allows for new meanings to emerge with each viewing experience.

Women's films screened at the right place to the right audience become meeting points where all three parties—director, character, and audience—communicate with each other (Figures 5.3 and 5.4). For instance, *Two Locks of Hair: The Lost Girls of Dersim*, which narrates the dreadful effects of the Dersim massacre, premiered in Dersim with the participation of women who had experienced the massacre and their daughters ("Tunceli'de, 'Dersim'in Kayıp Kızları' Belgeselinin Galası Yapıldı" 2014). Bingöl Elmas's *Pippa'ya Mektubum/My Letter to Pippa* (2010), which narrates the story of Pippa Bacca, a woman who was raped and murdered in Turkey while on a journey to spread a message of peace, was screened in eastern parts of Turkey, with the participation of Kurdish women's associations (Asmin Film 2010). Similarly, *The Play* was screened in thirty villages from Tarsus to Anamur for thirty days within the scope of a culture and art event held by the Mersin Metropolitan Municipality. Esmer states, "Those women [the Arslanköy village women's theatre group] brought their own experiences to other women who had similar experiences to them" (Esmer qouted in Fontini 2020; personal communication). In this way, the experiences of the women's theatre company reached villages where there are no roads, no water supply nor any visitors. Mizgin Müjde Arslan, who screened her film *A Fatal Dress: Polygamy* mostly for female audiences, says, "I cared women watched this

Figure 5.3 A village woman watching *The Play*. The still is from *Queen Lear*.

Figure 5.4 Two village women and a girl watching *The Play*. The still is from *Queen Lear*

story more and I loved our shared anger" (Fontini 2024b, 6). I find this sharing as a significant expression, a strong sensation. It shows us how individual stories become a part of a collective story.

I screened my films at international film festivals and women's film conferences. *Dream Workers* screened at the 29th International Adana Golden Boll Film Festival (2022) and the 15th Documentarist "Which Human Rights?" Film Festival (2022); *Filmin Adı Ne?/What's the Name of the Film?* screened at the 5th Taste of Anatolia Film Festival (2023), Doing Women's Film and Television History VI Conference (2023), and 59th International Antalya Golden Orange Film Festival (2022). Days before the screening of my films, I started worrying about how the narrative would be understood. Do the films give too many personal details? Are they tedious, or self-indulgent? I was preoccupied with being "misunderstood." Several months after the screening while writing this chapter, I understand one thing better: the meaning of the film does not only depend on the director and her intentions but also on the experience of the audience. As noted by Rancière, "Being a spectator is not some passive condition that we should transform into activity" (2009, 17). As spectators link what they see to what they have seen, said, done, and dreamed (2009, 17), they might understand things the director does not intend them to or they might not understand the things she wants them to. In this sense, being "misunderstood" is a part of the process. Misunderstanding some things might even be better than understanding the "right" things. "Whatever the person feels," says Ocean Voung, "I'd be satisfied as long as they leave the work with more of themselves" (2022). Now it is clear to me that filmmaking is not one-way communication from the filmmaker to the audience but a sharing. Sharing disrupts the hierarchical structure built by "giving and receiving" which reproduces the capitalist and patriarchal system. Sharing, in this sense, is a feminist intervention.

Conclusion: Filmmaking as a Form of Experience

Thinking about the potentiality of women's cinema, Umut Tümay Arslan asks a powerful question, "How do we learn to desire to see differently?" (U. T. Arslan 2022c). She is not asking about the ways through which we can see differently, she is asking about how to learn to want to see differently. This question is a life question. It asks about a becoming, an orientation, not a tactic or a strategy.

Continuing to think about women's cinema, Arslan says:

> The issue of women's cinema is not just a cinema issue. The struggle for how we should see, and how our view can change, is also the struggle for what will be the rational explanation of the world. The search for a better narrative and a better explanation of the world is an indispensable quest. Trying to change the stories about the world and our reality, both materially and in representation, is a task that we should aspire to, and although it may seem modest, it has the ability to transform. (U. T. Arslan 2022c)

Thinking together with Arslan, I understand that women's filmmaking in Turkey is experiential which means that it is an aspiration to see the world differently. Living life as a situation to be experienced and interacted with rather than as a problem to be solved leads the filmmakers of Women's New Cinema to observe, speak, and listen with care. The care here is not only about being attentive to the presence of the other but also knowing what one does not know which makes knowing possible. The attentive ears and eyes form the ethics of experiential filmmaking; female filmmakers develop a look that enacts the ethics of care for the experiences it captures. And the audiences, by choosing to watch their films, become active; their watching these films is a desire to see the world in another way, too. And although it may seem modest, these little changes have the ability to transform the world we experience every day.

Notes

1. "Because of Her, We Can" is the official theme of NAIDOC 2018, acknowledging and celebrating the contributions of Aboriginal and Torres Strait Islander women. To recognize and honor the power of the Anatolian women, I chose to adapt the title to my context.

2. I would like to thank Nalan Abbasoğlu for the insightful conversations we had on this new concept.
3. By calling the non-hierarchical space a place of feminist ethics, I am using the perspective of Umut Tümay Arslan (2019).
4. Here I am repeating the question posed by Rancière (2009, 12).

Chapter 6

Her Existence is Resistance: Being a Female Director in the Turkish Film Industry

I clearly remember the first time I met Handan İpekçi, an established female filmmaker from Turkey. It was after five-hour road trip from Istanbul to her home in Yeni Foça, a district of Izmir. The closer I got to her house over the bumpy roads, the more worried I became, constantly repeating the same question: "How can a filmmaker be inspired in this small town?" The town was empty, deserted, kind of sad, even heartbroken. Was it the town or was I feeling İpekçi?

Affected by the 12 September 1980 coup d'état, İpekçi made her first film, *Babam Askerde/Dad is in the Army* (1995). The only copy of the film was screened for one week and watched by nineteen people. Hoping to reach a broader audience, she decided she would distribute it herself, travelling to forty-five cities in one year. Her second film, *Büyük Adam Küçük Aşk/Big Man, Little Love* (2001) is a film on the Kurdish issue and because of this she had to deal with censorship and banning attempts. Her third film, *Hidden Faces*, addressed femicide and resulted in a huge financial debt that took seven years to pay off. She ended up making her fourth film, the commercial drama *Çınar Ağacı/The Plane Tree* (2011), in order to be able to continue repaying the debt. Her extraordinary story of producing her films—raising funding, directing as well as organizing distribution and screenings—provides a unique example of how female directors from Turkey struggle to make their films within the country's monopolized industry and tense political atmosphere.

The first aim of this chapter is to understand the dynamics of the sector that directly affect filmmakers, such as production, funding, screening, and censorship. To do this, I apply a contextual approach and simultaneously analyze the political, economic, cultural, and social events that impact the mode of production. The second aim is to determine the particular ways these dynamics affect female directors (e.g., gender-based discrimination, international accessibility, and the visibility of female directors) and to understand if being a female director brings its own troubles and adds to the ongoing sectoral problems.

As tangible and lived realities, these industrial dynamics affect the aesthetics, style, and narratives of female filmmakers. By examining these dynamics, I illuminate how these female filmmakers produce while working within the Turkish film industry, despite the monopolized dynamics of the industry which also shapes their discourse. Analyzing the impact of the tense sociopolitical atmosphere on the cultural production also helps me to reveal why these female filmmakers produce the films they do at this particular time in history.

I divide this chapter into three parts and allocate each section to one main funding body: state funding, Eurimages[1] and festivals, and personal investment. In these sections, I discuss İpekçi's production methods as well as the filmmaking practices of other contemporary female filmmakers from Turkey. This analysis examines how Women's New Cinema addresses the ongoing sectoral problems and how its discourse is affected by political and cultural dynamics.

Cultural Ministry, Censorship, and Misogyny

The funding the Cultural Ministry developed in 1990 is the only state funding available in the Turkish film industry. The Cinema Support Board was formed to coordinate this funding and its members change every two years. As stated in the guidelines of the Ministry, "The Cinema Support Board consists of a representative of the Ministry, one member chosen from among the members of the relevant field professional associations, and three members to be determined by the Ministry, who are experts in the fields related to cinema" (T. C. Kültür ve Turizm Bakanlığı 2004). This funding largely supports independent films which are unable to sustain themselves through box office revenue. For instance, between 2005 and 2013, 587 feature films were produced in Turkey and the Cultural Ministry provided financial support to 282 of them; that is, 50 per cent of all the films produced (Kanzler 2014, 8, 18). However, in most cases, the average amount of finance provided by the Ministry is not enough to meet the entire budget to produce and release a feature film in Turkey. İpekçi's struggles vividly depict this fact. During my interview with her, she said:

> I got the first funding from the Cultural Ministry, but I had to apply to Eurimages because the support from the Cultural Ministry was not enough to complete a film. I had no experience in applying for such funds. I knew that Seçkin Yasar had applied to Eurimages previously. Biket İlhan and Seçkin Yasar's experiences were quite beneficial while I prepared my application . . . The support from Eurimages was very helpful. Without it, the support from the Cultural Ministry alone could only be enough to make half of the film . . . That's how I made the film [*Big Man, Little Love*]; a coproduction of Hungary, Greece and Turkey. (İpekçi quoted in Fontini 2020; personal communication)

İpekçi receiving help from the other female directors such as İlhan and Yasar is evidence of female solidarity within the industry. But her experience shows clearly that the directors have to come up with other solutions to fully fund their films. The majority of films constituting Women's New Cinema have received support from the Cultural Ministry; for example: *Nobody's Home*, *İz/The Trace* (Ustaoğlu, 1994), *Clair Obscur*, *Somewhere in Between*, *What Remains*, *Fakat Müzeyyen Bu Derin Bir Tutku*, *Queen Lear*, *Lifelong*, *Dust Cloth*, *Başka Dilde Aşk/Love in Another Language* (Başarır, 2009), *Until I Lose My Breath*, *Zephyr*, *Something Useful*, *Motherland*, *Evcilik/Playing House* (Elmas, 2012) and *Mamak'ta* (Türk, 2010). However, most of these films, such as *Clair Obscur*, *Queen Lear*, *Dust Cloth*, *Lifelong*, *Until I Lose My Breath*, *Zephyr*, *Motherland*, and *Something Useful*, also received support from international funding bodies. This funding system makes independent cinema in Turkey dependent on the Cultural Ministry. However, this mechanism also enables female directors to collaborate with international co-producers, making their cinema transnational. I describe the details of this feature in the next section.

The Cultural Ministry provides both refundable and non-refundable funding. If a film cannot meet certain criteria, the producer might need to give the funding back (Fontini 2017, 101). This would put the filmmakers in an incredible amount of debt. The experiences of İpekçi attest to the pressure this refund system places upon filmmakers. Upon finishing her third film, *Hidden Faces*, she became one of the directors who was asked to pay their funding back:

> When they asked for the money back, I applied to the administrative court for a stay of execution. I lost the case. Then, I applied to the Council of State. I lost the case again. 190 thousand liras rose to 550 thousand liras with the statutory interest. To solve the financial problem with *Hidden Faces*, I applied to the fund with *The Plane Tree*. So, *The Plane Tree* was a movie made to make money. Meanwhile, a tax amnesty was introduced. 550 thousand liras were cut down and split into instalments. It is a long story, which actually deserves its own movie. (İpekçi quoted in Fontini 2020; personal communication)

İpekçi speculates that she experienced this nightmare-like process because her previous film, *Big Man Little Love*, was on the Kurdish issue. Her daring to make such a film, especially as a *female* director, in an era when it was not permitted to talk about the Kurdish issue, "deserved" punishment (İpeçi quoted in Fontini 2017, 349–50).

Yeşim Ustaoğlu, one of the most prominent directors of Women's New Cinema, experienced a similar situation. She made *Clair Obscur* with the support of the Cultural Ministry. To be able to screen her film, she had to be evaluated and categorized by the ministry. Because of the sex scenes, the Ministry categorized the film as +18. Under this categorization, Ustaoğlu would need to pay the support back. Ustaoğlu shortened the sex scenes, and that is how the film was excluded from the +18 category (Yaşartürk 2017). As seen in this example, the Ministry indirectly influences the content of the films.

Kanzler explains that "Turkey belongs to the small number of European countries which have chosen to provide support for film-related activities directly through a government department rather than to create a distinct body" (2014, 23). As stated in the guidelines of the Ministry, it is the Cinema Support Board, which consists of a representative of Ministry and other members determined by the Ministry, who decides which films to provide funding to (T. C. Kültür ve Turizm Bakanlığı 2004). The same Ministry also evaluates the content of them as well as categorizing them and choosing whether or not to provide the license necessary to screen them. The guidelines of the Ministry state that

> film, video and musical works are not allowed to be shown and performed if they pose a threat to the indivisible integrity of the state with its territory and nation, national sovereignty, republic, national security, public order, general security, public interest, general morality, general health; if they contain the elements of incitement to crime, be contrary to foreign policy, not suitable for our national culture, customs, and traditions. (Kültür ve Turizm Bakanlığı Teftiş Kurulu Başkanlığı 1986)

It means that the Ministry might not approve the content of the film if it is not suitable for "our national culture, customs and traditions." *Kurak Günler/Burning Days* (Alper, 2022) might be a good example to understand how this guideline can be implemented. After the film had its world premiere at the Cannes Film Festival, media channels close to the Turkish government criticized the film harshly over the queer elements of the narrative and a lynch campaign started in social media. The Cultural Ministry requested back the financial production support given to the film due to the "script revisions" made during the development stage. The producer Nadir Öperli and the director Emin Alper released a statement emphasizing that script development is a natural practice during the years-long production process of a film, adding that there is no such scenario change supervision in any democratic country in the world. They also mention that this decision, taken just before the release of the film, is a censorship practice (*Bianet* 2022).

In Turkey, films that are not even made can be punished. Çiğdem Mater, a female producer, was sentenced to imprisonment "for a film that was not shot" (Altyazı Fasikül 2023). The main accusation against Mater is that "she was trying to raise financing for a documentary project about the Gezi Park movement—a film which was never made" (*International Coalition for Filmmakers at Risk* 2022). Two days after the verdict was announced, Susma Bitsin (Speak Up To End), a feminist solidarity network established by women to combat sexual harassment and discrimination in film, television and theatre industries, released a statement in support of Mater:

> We shall not remain silent against injustice! We stand in solidarity with Çiğdem Mater. At the recent Gezi trial in which Çiğdem Mater was also trialed, we once again witnessed how resisting the patriarchal government and its oppression, and refusing to submit to lawlessness is punished. We know this punishment is a consequence of fear and fury, and yet the voices of millions shall not be silenced. You have punished a film that hasn't been shot yet; we will not stop making our films and fighting for what we know is just. We know the darkness will end once we end our silence. (*Susma Bitsin* 2022)

I am unable to find a vocabulary that can finalize this paragraph, knowing that Mater is in a prison cell in Istanbul at the moment. I will just repeat the hashtag created by Susma Bitsin Platform: #westandwithÇiğdemMater

State funding channels, especially in authoritarian states, are expected to implement an invisible censorship mechanism and produce self-censorship, as in the case of Turkey. Film festival coordinator, critic, and producer Yamaç Okur suggests that recent films are under greater scrutiny. He states that "no film that criticizes state or government policies on any matter can get funding, nor can films that problematize the conditions of marginalized groups such as LGBTI+, religious minorities (other than Sunni), or the Kurdish question" (Okur quoted in Akkaya 2016, 70–1). Barış Saydam illustrates Okur's perspective by giving an example of the ministry's approach to Kurdish films: "All Kurdish films that received state support recently are films that try to find a 'middle way', do not contain rhetoric and criticism, and tell relatively more naive human stories. However, the Cultural Ministry does not support 'harsh' political films such as the ones produced by Kazım Öz, and Özcan Alper that make more direct criticism" (2021, 6). The experiences of Çayan Demirel and Ertuğrul Mavioğlu, who made *Bakur/North* (2015), clearly show the "tendencies" of the Cultural Ministry. *North* is "a documentary that invites its audience to reflect on a war that has been continuing for decades and gives an insightful look on its main subject, the PKK"[2] (Surela Film 2015). As the film deals with a "harsh" issue, the Cultural Ministry chose not provide the film with a registration license, which prevented it from being screened at the 34th International Istanbul Film Festival (T24 2015). *Zer* (Öz, 2017) is another Kurdish film being supported and at the same time censored by the Cultural Ministry. The film "tells the story of a young man

Jan (Nik Xhelilaj) who embarks on a journey to Turkey after his grandmother Zarife passes away with cancer in a New York hospital. Through the story of Zarife, the film broaches the subject of the 1938 massacre of Kurds in Dersim, and the erasure of the event from Turkish official history" (Grgic 2017). Some scenes of the film were found "inconvenient" by the Ministry. Instead of cutting those scenes, the director chose to incorporate a black title card on which is written: "You cannot watch this scene because it was found inconvenient by the General Directorate of Cinema of the Ministry of Culture and Supervisory Board" (V. Aydemir 2017). İpekçi experienced similar censorship with her film *Big Man, Little Love*, which problematizes the Kurdish issue:

> The film was being screened at Turkish stand of the Cannes Film Festival. Its Turkish name is *Big Man, Little Love* and international name is *Big Man, Little Love, Hejar*. The name Hejar became a problem, such a meaningless problem. Five months after its release, they [the Cultural Ministry] decided to re-evaluate the film. Such a decision has never been made in Turkish cinema history before. And the film was banned. I went to the court, I won the case in a month; the film was re-released. (İpekçi quoted in Fontini 2020; personal communication)

It was the name Hejar, a female name in the Kurdish language, that became a problem. Indeed, this problem promoted the film and raised public attention. It was scheduled to leave theatres but the controversy worked in its favor and its cinematic release was extended. Approximately 35,000 more people watched the film thanks to the intervention of the Ministry (İpekçi quoted in Fontini 2020; personal communication). Zeynep Dadak, who chose to immigrate to Germany to continue her filmmaking in a better financial and mental state of mind, brings a different perspective to understanding the relationship of filmmakers from Turkey with censorship mechanisms. During the interview I made with her, she said:

> We were so marginalized politically that neither of my films received support from the Cultural Ministry. I don't have the human power to struggle with them, to undergo all that fight. I am using the power I have to create, to continue creating . . . But as a person who has actively written for 20 years, I can say that it is the first time I wrote so freely [in Berlin], without being afraid of losing things . . . The pressure you feel is not only a pressure but something you fight with, it determines our emotions, our fears, it intervenes with what we do and what we don't do; this is what we call auto-censorship. And we all, without recognizing it, have been censoring ourselves for a very long time. (Dadak quoted in Fontini 2020; personal communication)

The authoritarian mechanism places pressures on individuals and institutions to determine who says what and how. As stated by Dadak, this results in film-makers censoring themselves without even recognizing it. As it is not possible to understand the direct effects of auto-censorship, we do not know the untold stories and the increate characters of Women's New Cinema. But, as mentioned by the female filmmakers, this unproductive funding mechanism influences their narratives and production processes. Another example from Ceylan Özgün Özçelik depicts the picture from a slightly different angle. Her words reflect how the state, its governing bodies and their authoritarian policies regulate the sociocultural order:

> It wasn't the government censoring the films but one of the members of the audience standing up and talking for a long time about the moral problems of it and then complaining about it to a newspaper. So, what is more problematic and horrifying is that it's everyone around you is some kind of an agent of some dark power . . . It feels like we are always being watched, someone always watches us, it's as if you are losing it . . . In our houses, out in the streets, we hear voices. The voices of constructions, the voices of the president, the municipals, the voices of newswomen, anchormen. Every voice is violence. Every voice affects us. (Berlinale Talents 2017)

As stated by the directors of Women's New Cinema, the films and the freedom of the directors are directly affected by the authoritarian tendencies of the state and society. It is difficult to be an independent filmmaker in Turkey, criticizing the state and its policies but at the same time needing the funding that comes directly from the state's governing body to continue making films. But there is a worse case than being an *independent* filmmaker in Turkey, which is to be a *female independent* filmmaker in Turkey.

Most of the female directors interviewed for this book made similar remarks about the male-dominated structure of the Cinema Support Board. For instance, Dadak, who made her first feature-length film together with another female director, Merve Kayan, says that they heard people saying, "Two women? I don't know . . . Maybe two women can make one decent filmmaker." She continued, "There are gatekeepers dominant in film criticism and funding bodies . . . Full of mansplaining. Who can make a film? Who deserves to make the film? Who should make the film? There is this mechanism, in that systematic flow" (Dadak quoted in Fontini 2020; personal communication). As stated by Dadak, it is an entirely male-centric system in which men decide that men can make films, men deserve to make the films, men should make the films. Mizgin Müjde Arslan, another filmmaker of Women's New Cinema, has had similar experiences that support Dadak's statement:

> The production companies, organizations, the Cultural Ministry didn't take me seriously. Neither in my first film, nor in the second, third, fourth . . . You make the first film, and it shows that you are serious, you are decisive, you have the talent; you think it will be easier now, but it never became easier for me. Although I finished the films, although I screened them at festivals, men in suits never took me seriously. It was mostly because I am a woman. There could be other factors, but the primary factor was my being a woman, as our male colleagues are more comfortable [with other men]. They are luckier in communication, opening the doors, reaching the means of production. It is as if there is a percentage allocated to women, they say, "Sure, women should be included in our festival, but their number shouldn't exceed 10 percent." It is about seeming diverse, we are an ornament, a colour. (Fontini 2024b, 8)

As underlined by Arslan, it is not about including women but seeming to include women. Sure, they are inviting women to apply for funding but does being invited mean that you are really wanted?[3]

One of the direct results of such gender-based discrimination is that the female directors of Women's New Cinema cannot make films as frequently as male directors do. The first two decades of the 2000s saw an increase in the number of female directors bringing new visions and ideas to the cinematic realm in Turkey, but most of these directors have managed to make only one film to date. The female directors of Women's New Cinema receive less support at home than male directors do, but why do so many female directors make only one film? Who receives money? Dadak replies:

> These certain structures work only for some directors in Turkey. He takes the support from the Cultural Ministry and then finds a co-producer. This is not the case for us. I am sure many female directors who started making films after the 2000s are not less talented than the male directors. But if you don't have brothers or sisters backing you up, you are all alone by yourself in this journey . . . Especially for us who started making films after the 2010s . . . We didn't learn how to produce a film from a previous generation. Both the gender-biased perception and the political segregation prevented us from producing . . . For instance, my primary producer is in Germany now. I wish I could make films in Turkey. I will, but it is very difficult to find financial support in Turkey. (Dadak quoted in Fontini 2020; personal communication)

We need more women and LGBTI+ decision-makers in the industry because who has the power to make the decision does affect the norm, the discourse, the "reality." In some historic moments, some people have more power to speak on some issues. As observed in the history of cinema in Turkey, it was mostly male directors who constructed female representation throughout the 20th century. This resulted in a stereotypical female character type characterized by her passivity, silence, obedience, and sacrifice.[4] The discourse developed by the directors of Women's New Cinema disrupts this order. That is why we need to talk about their issues, we need to tell their stories, as their stories are the stories of male-headed institutions. We need to talk to subvert this order. We need to talk because no one else does.

European Funding Channels and Orientalism

As described in the previous section, the Cultural Ministry is the only state funding that provides support to some independent productions; however, the amount provided is typically not enough to make a feature-length film. So, independent directors need European funding. Previously the primary source of European funding was from Eurimages. However, this is no longer the case as funding is now available from other European sources such as the World Cinema Fund, Balkan Fund, and Hubert Bals Fund, which support both male and female independent directors.

So far, many female directors have developed their projects thanks to support from these international funding channels. For instance, Handan İpekçi's *Hidden Faces* received the Script Development Fund from the Thessaloniki International Film Festival (2004), Yeşim Ustaoğlu's *Journey to the Sun* received the Script Development Fund from the Montpellier Film Festival (1995). Aslı Özge's film *Lifelong* and Emine Emel Balcı's film *Until I Lose My Breath* were supported by Eurimages, while Ahu Öztürk's *Dust Cloth* received postproduction funding from the Hamburg Film Fund. Belma Baş's *Zephyr* and Pelin Esmer's *Something Useful* both received support from the Hubert Bals Fund, Senem Tüzen's *Motherland* was supported by Germany's Connecting Cottbus coproduction market and the Thessaloniki Film Festival Crossroads co-production forum, and Melisa Önel's *Seaburners* received money from the Thessaloniki Film Festival Agora Works in Progress fund. Berke Baş's *Hush!* and Bingöl Elmas's *My Letter to Pippa* were supported by Arte.

These independent channels not only provide support for the directors to develop their films but also provide them with a space to screen their films. In this current cultural environment, blockbusters dominate Turkish theatres. The old cinematheques are being replaced with high-tech multiplexes located in shopping malls and the distribution and exhibition of films in Turkey are monopolized (Ş. Aydemir et al. 2016). And independent films "become the guests in their own houses" (Kırel, 2004). Film festivals therefore are often the only spaces for independent films to meet their audiences. As Turkish academic Serpil Kırel argues, "Festivals are the refuges of national cinemas, which have lost their 'aura' in the face of Hollywood" (2004, 119). However, in the Turkish context, festivals might decide not to host certain films. They might end up cancelling themselves so there will be no venue to attend even as a guest.

The 60th International Antalya Golden Orange Film Festival, one of the most prestigious film festivals in Turkey, was cancelled in 2023 after controversy over a documentary film *Kanun Hükmü/The Decree* (2023) made by the female filmmaker Nejla Demirci. The festival including the film in the National Documentary Film category removed the film days before the festival took place. To oppose this censorship attempt, jury members and filmmakers decided not to attend the festival. To calm the tense atmosphere, the festival decided to take the film back. In response to this, the Cultural Ministry and the official sponsors decided not to support the festival. In the end, the festival was cancelled altogether. An entire festival was censored so as not to screen a film that talks about a "taboo": the consequences of the failed anti-Erdoğan coup on ordinary people. As I discussed in the first chapter, in Turkey, one needs to know where to talk and where to stay silent in order to be welcomed. But the filmmakers of Women's New Cinema such as Demirci remain stubborn at the expense of becoming the unwanted.

When they are not cancelled, international film festivals can also provide space for independent films to guarantee they will be shown on the international market. Most of the films of Women's New Cinema are screened at national and international film festivals, making their cinema a transnational cinema. As stated by academic and author Patricia White (2015), women's films circulating through international festivals not only connects the films with their audiences and increases their accessibility but it also transforms the aesthetic and contextual values of art cinema, challenging the feminist genealogies and decolonizing the festivals.

However, the expectations of these international funding and screening bodies can be questionable. Up until 2010, the main mission of Eurimages was "to support works which reflect the multiple facets of a European society whose common roots are evidence of a single culture" (Yılmazok 2010, 89). The sentiment of this statement is problematic over its stereotyping expectation even for a country that sees itself within the European zone, but it complicates the problem more for a country like Turkey that can situate itself neither in Europe nor in the East, Asia, or the Middle East.[5] The feelings of prominent filmmaker Ali Özgentürk help us understand the problem better as it provides an example of how the stereotyping expectations of Western funding institutions affect non-European artists:

> How do they view Turkish artists? Will my films be watched only when I tell something about the Kurds? I felt this, Westerners made me feel this. I got awards . . . But I don't know if I had shot an adaptation of Dostoyevsky, and

> if I had shot it well, it would still be welcomed. I don't know how it would be greeted if I shot an adaptation of Shakespeare. (Zaim 2008, 44)

It complicates the problem even further for female directors and their female subjects when we think about the socioreligious facts of Turkey. As discussed broadly in Chapter 3, the "Islamic women of the Middle East are typically seen as victims of religion, patriarchy, tradition, and poverty in the West, women artists from the same region are expected to testify to this presumed condition" (Amireh and Majaj quoted in Suner 2007, 65–6). These assumptions and perspectives can lead female directors to create stereotyped Middle Eastern female images in order to obtain financial support. Applying for European funding may mean being denied a plural identity for these women artists from the Middle East. Making films due to international funding but despite its expectations is a difficult dilemma experienced by many Middle Eastern filmmakers. European funding is more important than ever for independent female directors in today's Turkey because of the unfair and censoring public funding mechanism but external funding for these directors has its own impact on their output, according to the values, tastes and assumptions of the funders.

One last problem worth mentioning in this section is that it is often the male cinematographer or the male producer who takes the credit for festival screenings, achievements, and awards. Turkish cinema history is filled with such examples. When Füruzan and Gülsün Karamustafa's film *My Cinemas* was shown at the Cannes Film Festival, film critics such as Atilla Dorsay gave the entire credit to another critic, Mehmet Basutçu, who praised the film to the festival coordinators (Fontini 2017, 163). Another example comes from the critic Kerem Akça, who criticized the selection of the Istanbul Film Festival committee, whose head was Pelin Esmer, a prominent director of Women's New Cinema, with such words: "At #istfilmfest18, the committee awarded the weakest film of the festival *Borç*. From this award, we can understand that Pelin Esmer who proved that she is nothing without her cinematographer Tiryaki tries to create new Pelin Esmers" (Akça 2018). Here, Akça degrades Esmer's successes by praising her male cinematographer, Tiryaki. Azra Deniz Okyay, an emerging director of Women's New Cinema who won the Venice Critics Week Prize at the Venice Film Festival with her debut film, *Hayaletler/Ghosts* (2020), also suggests that there is a gender bias from male film critics:

> I feel so lucky that I didn't have a male producer when we were awarded at Antalya Film Festival or else they would think that it is because of him . . . I am sure they would think in this way. Although our film [*Ghosts*] received

> most of the awards in the last two years, I am reading things like "Give them an Oscar as well!" just because I am a female director. (DW Turkey 2021)

The film critics are not only omitting women from history by dismissing their achievements and by recording only the stories of male directors as history but they also make the male crew responsible for women's achievements, assigning agency to men and again erasing the visibility of women. Such omissions are not specific to Turkey. For instance, Susanne Bier, a female filmmaker from Denmark, was "overshadowed by the notoriety accorded the Dogme 95 'brothers.'" Despite becoming one of the first directors to successfully employ the Dogma 95 manifesto to her films and receive an Oscar (for *Hævnen/In a Better World*, 2010), most critics disregarded her success (White 2015, 6). Although one of the most prominent features of the fifth-generation Chinese cinema and recent sub-Saharan African cinema is the female protagonist having self-determination, female directors contributing to these movements are "much less well known internationally and receive less support at home" (2015, 6). As seen, the misogynistic attitudes of the patriarchal film industry continue to affect women's cinema worldwide.

Personal Investment

Since funding from the Cultural Ministry alone is often not enough to make a film, movies are produced by combining the funding from the Cultural Ministry and festivals (Saydam 2021, 8). Additionally, most of the time, the directors invest personally in their productions. For instance, Çağan Irmak produces commercial movies so he can invest his income in making art-house films. Reha Erdem shoots advertisements so he can afford to make films as he wants. Similarly, Uğur Yücel works as an actor in television series to raise money to produce his films (2021, 8). Additionally, most of the time, low-budget films are financed through deferrals of the filmmaker, producer or screenwriter fees (Kanzler 2014, 12).

Although the directors are in more need than ever of national funding channels, the existing ones are threatened with being shut down, such as Anadolu Kültür (Anatolian Culture), because of the political agenda. Zeynep Dadak evaluates this point from the perspective of female producers:

> The biggest failure of Turkish cinema is . . . the films cannot give birth to themselves. Without making money, how many films can a producer produce? I know so many talented people but all of them, including myself, need to do a second, a third job . . . There are very few people who enjoy

> making their films and make money out of them. This is almost impossible for independent films. I wish everyone earned the money they deserve and continued making their films. The industry has many young, talented female producers but the question is if they can continue. (Dadak quoted in Fontini 2020; personal communication)

And as seen in the case of many films made by contemporary female directors, these limitations shape their processes, even their narratives, and styles. But as Belmin Söylemez says, "Women push the limits . . . without aiming for an ideal feature-length or an ideal fiction, without setting standard goals, women can say, 'I'll make a movie'" (Söylemez quoted in Fontini, 2020; personal communication). These words reflect not only my experience but also the experiences of many other contemporary female filmmakers. They push the limits, and they work on their dreams.

Conclusion: Solidarity, Now!

Although digital platforms offer alternative venues where independent films can find audiences, this still presents a problem. How does an independent director get the audience to see her films in the plethora of content on the world wide web? Under the control of an authoritarian state which has neoliberalist, misogynistic, radical conservative tendencies, the circulated cultural products are apolitical and monolithic. The audience is pushed into multiplexes to see films that are either imported blockbusters or domestic blockbusters, as the distribution and exhibition are monopolized, in between buying clothes and accessories. There has never been a self-sustaining independent art-house cinema in Turkish film history because, as I have discussed in this chapter, the industry never invested in itself so never provided the filmmakers with proper infrastructure. With the Cultural Ministry as the only major source of funding from the government, female and dissentient filmmakers are left with no decent support for production, distribution and exhibition.

Yet, the problem is not simply a cultural one. The state implements its own strategy to generate an entirely new society whose values are completely different from the previous one. This is a systematic attempt to create a "new Turkey."[6] But, as Nuri Bilge Ceylan explains, "When the artist cannot tolerate and endure anymore, s/he starts producing as cinema promises emancipation from an allegedly inevitable destiny" (Ceylan quoted in Yetişkin 2010, 113). These words reveal the connection between the current cultural and sociopolitical situation in Turkey and our filmmaking practice. Women continue making films as a strategy to exist and resist. They have more need than ever for funding from international agencies (festivals, funders, distributors, and producers) to sustain themselves and their filmmaking practice; it is these international industry circles that need to show solidarity with them now. Supporting non-Western women's filmmaking practices creates a more feminist and decolonized film industry worldwide. This chapter focused on these discussions and problems because it is only by resolving such complications that female filmmakers from Turkey can remain independent.

Notes

1. Eurimages is a cultural support fund of the Council of Europe.
2. The PKK is the Kurdistan Workers' Party. Because of their separatist ideology, they are considered a terrorist organization by Turkish state.
3. I learned from Sara Ahmed to question the relationship between the invitation and the real intention.
4. Chapter 2 discusses the particularities of this female character.
5. Films produced in Turkey also cannot be classified easily; while some festivals accept submissions from Turkey under the East European category, others evaluate Turkey as a Middle Eastern country.
6. I discuss the particularities of this "new Turkey" in Chapter 1.

Afterword: Filmmaking is Not a Luxury

Realizing this project was a vital necessity for me so that our stories would not be omitted from history. As Adrienne Rich reminds us:

> Whatever is unnamed, undepicted in images, whatever is omitted from biography, censored in collections of letters, whatever is misnamed as something else, made difficult-to-come-by, whatever is buried in the memory by the collapse of meaning under an inadequate or lying language—this will become, not merely unspoken, but unspeakable. (Rich 1977, 6)

Similarly, the flourishing of women's cinema in Turkey is vital too because the social, cultural and political dynamics prevent us from hoping, whereas Women's New Cinema is about insisting on a better world.

Contemporary female filmmakers in Turkey realize the "impossible" and the "necessary" (see Hartman quoted in Bulley 2020) by attempting a feminist film culture under a restrictive regime. The feminist in this feminist film culture is Sara Ahmed's kind which understands feminism as a "sensible reaction to the injustices of the world" (Ahmed quoted in Mehra 2017). Contemporary women's filmmaking in Turkey is not about creating a counter-discourse to the male gaze or an oppositional cinema against the patriarchal one but it is a sensible reaction to the injustices of the country. It is a critical response to the intertwined racist, heterosexual, capitalistic, and patriarchal norms and our ongoing investment and participation in them. In this sense, women filmmakers from Turkey attempt "to change the frame" rather than "want[ing] to be in the frame" (U. T. Arslan 2022b). What they do here is "to imagine another frame, to transform the frame, the staging, the established seeing and hearing mechanism, and to build different perspectives on ourselves and each other from the masculine perspective" (2022b). That is how contemporary women's filmmaking provides us with a space away from the dominant visual norms and the violence they imply.

Women's New Cinema re-centralizes Turkey's cinema by decentering from the gaze of white, heterosexual men. It attempts to focus on the diverse experiences of women through decolonized lenses. The experience here, again, is not about including Kurdish women, Muslim women, transexual women, Alevi women, poor women, or Armenian and Greek women within the frame but "to rethink and question what life and politics mean in terms of being Kurdish, Armenian, a transgender woman, or a poor woman" (U. T. Arslan 2022c). So far, we have been taught "either to ignore our differences or to view them as causes for separation and suspicion rather than as forces to change . . . But community must not mean a shedding of our differences, nor the pathetic pretense that these differences do not exist" (Lorde [1984] 2007, 112). Women's New Cinema attempts a feminist community, through "encounters, often even uncomfortable and unsettling ones, that compel us to move with differences rather than suppressing them" (U. T. Arslan 2022c). Through women's films, we can confront our own and each other's differences. "When we look at our differences and not allow ourselves to be divided, when we own them and are not divided by them, that is when we will be able to move on" (Lorde and Baldwin, 1984). To move on is about imagining new ways of realizing ourselves and coexistence. This act of imagination is a radical act; it is the first step toward change.

In her inspiring essay "Poetry is Not a Luxury," Audre Lorde says:

> For women, then, poetry is not a luxury. It is a vital necessity of our existence. It forms the quality of the light within which we predicate our hopes and dreams toward survival and change, first made into language, then into idea, then into more tangible action (Lorde 2017b, 8).[1]

Thinking on Lorde's words, I come to an understanding of women's filmmaking, especially in Turkey, not as a luxury but as a form of communication, an interaction, even solidarity. Women's filmmaking is "a vital necessity of our existence" and a space of radical possibility.

Note

1. I would like to thank Dr Rebecca Hill for drawing my attention to this point.

Epilogue

In this section, using the extracts from the interviews I made with contemporary female directors, I will attempt to reveal their stories from their own voices. I talked with each director (Yeşim Ustaoğlu, Pelin Esmer, Belmin Söylemez, Mizgin Müjde Arslan, Zeynep Dadak, and Handan İpekçi) for around two hours but it is not possible to cover all the topics we discussed here. That is why I extracted only the answers that I believe can provide us with an understanding of their life and filmmaking experiences, imaginations, and insights while knowing that it will only be a partial understanding. However, the glimpse this epilogue provides us can still tell us a lot about being a creative woman in contemporary Turkey. Listening to the willful stories of these directors and learning about the possibilities they created for themselves might even inspire us to imagine what used to be impossible.

Mizgin Müjde Arslan was born in Göllü village in Mardin (a city in southeastern Turkey).[1] Not only because of being raised by her grandparents but also because of the conservative norms of the society she was born into, she experienced a difficult childhood. I started our dialogue by asking a question about Arslan's girlhood. Pınar Fontini: *I would like to start with your birthplace. You were born in Göllü village in Mardin. How did it feel to be a child there?*

Mizgin Müjde Arslan: *This is a bit difficult to understand. There were some impossible situations where all the doors were closed in your face, and you were at a dead end . . . Nobody in our village would continue their education. After primary school, girls would prepare their dowries and get married in a couple of years. They were appreciated for their skills in cleaning, cooking, and dowry crafts. And I still don't know today who I was inspired by, but there was one thing on my mind: I had to attend middle school. I believed that if I did, I would be able to further my education. I didn't like the story my grandmother and aunts had written for me. I didn't want to be a woman like that. I was able to stay sane for only one reason. I mean, I can't find any other explanation. The reason was I could write, dream, aim for something, and have the desire to tell. When I was young, I was certain that I would survive. I would survive and tell my story. I would tell my story to the world. I was so ambitious. I didn't want to go back to the village or Mardin to tell my story. One day, I would tell it to the whole world. We need to write more stories about women, focusing on women's experiences. All women like you and me . . . We should all do it without being a perfectionist. We need to embrace our imperfections, make more films, and be more visible.*

As Arslan said, we need to talk about and externalize our experiences as women. It is really valuable to be able to do the things that have been repressed and kept inside us due to being a woman in society and a daughter of a family. Her journey, therefore, is quite inspiring. Like Arslan, Handan İpekçi had a difficult life story. Her story is also a stubborn story. Pınar Fontini: *How did you decide to become a director?*

Handan İpekçi: *I got married when I was in my second year at university. The school was in Ankara and I came to Istanbul. I thought I would come back from Istanbul and finish school, but I got married in '76 and had a child in '78. That's why I couldn't go to school. I could not go back to Ankara or take the exams, so I was dismissed. And ten years passed. Meanwhile, the 1980 coup happened. After these ten years, I asked myself, "What are you doing?" Cleaning, cooking, looking after the kids . . . I ended up a traditional housewife, which I did not like at all. I did not want to be like that and made a decision. I graduated from the university and started working as an assistant director. After I went to Ankara to finish the school, my marriage ended. Afterwards, I asked myself a lot, "Could I have been a director if I had stayed married?" I thought that it would have been really hard, or maybe impossible for me to be a director.*

How similar Arslan's and İpekçi's stories are to that of Virginia Woolf, who needed to kill the Angel in her house to be able to write. The particularities of this Angel can be found in the introduction of this book. She is a phantom living under the same roof with Woolf and she keeps reminding her of the duties of a sacrificing housewife, the perfect mother. To be able to realize herself for real, as an author, Woolf understands that she has to kill the Angel. Similar to Woolf, Arslan, and İpekçi recognize that they need to leave damaging familial ties behind to be able to start making films. Women filmmakers try different ways to realize themselves and make their art. Arslan, for instance, kills the Angel by revealing the secrets of her/our house(s) in her films. In a striking scene in *I Flew You Stayed*, Arslan confronts her mother in front of the camera. Pınar Fontini: *Turning the camera to yourself breaks the togetherness, leads you to disclose yourself, and breaks the silence. It basically lets you come forward in the community and tell others that you have a different story.*

Mizgin Müjde Arslan: *I had to do it. No matter how painful it was. Nobody wants to say they have problems in their families. They usually want to show the good side. They want to look good. People tend to tell good stories about their happy childhood. But no, I lived those things. And I needed to tell them, share them. As for happy childhoods people tend to tell.*

Pınar Fontini: *I, for one, didn't have a very happy childhood. Maybe that's why I was able to identify with you. You went through sad things as a little girl. Maybe I felt represented. It is really important for some of us to be able to say that they were unhappy. It makes what we do real, sincere and authentic. At the end of your film [*I Flew You Stayed*], you ask your mother why she did not take you with her. It is a big question, a big confrontation. And you're doing it on camera. It is already so hard. Doesn't it make it even harder?*

Mizgin Müjde Arslan: *You're right. It was a heavy confrontation. It is a difficult question to ask, one that shapes your whole life and you will keep asking all through your life. The confrontation scene really moved me during the editing and still moves me when I watch the film. I still tear up and may even cry if I can. But it is a scene which also empowers me. I needed to approach the issue even though it hurt. Just like with many issues. And the question still remains for me. I still have not got the answer to the question why they left me.*

In this scene, Arslan asks her mother why she left her behind when she moved to Iraq with Arslan's brother. Her mother tells her some things but these things do not erase the question from Arslan's life. Similarly, Yeşim Ustaoğlu confronts us with difficult questions, the nightmares of the past and present. For instance, the main character of *Somewhere in Between* is Zehra, who struggles to live her life despite being stuck in a small town with her family; it is Ayşe/Eleni in *Waiting for the Clouds* who dares to remember her past, her identity as a Greek woman; and it is Mehmet in *Journey to the Sun* who explores the meaning/politics of being a Kurd living in Turkey upon the death of his Kurdish friend, Berzan. Pınar Fontini: *You have told us the stories of various characters so far. As far as I know, you started to write* Journey to The Sun *after seeing a news report on a newspaper clipping. What led you to tell us the story of Elmas in* Clair Obscur? *Or how did* Somewhere in Between *come about?*

Yeşim Ustaoğlu: *Yes, as you said, I started out from two newspaper clippings and wrote* Journey to the Sun. *I was impacted by the events like submerging [of Kurdish villages] or cross signs [on minority people's doors]. My purpose at the time was to investigate the tendency in the Western regions [of Turkey] to go on with life by turning a blind eye or pretending not to see. I wanted to explore an instance of migration in the opposite direction. I wanted to go back to the place people usually left. It was part of the course of events. As for* Waiting for the Clouds, *it was a period I drifted apart from Trabzon [a city in the north of Turkey]. But it was always on my mind. I spent my childhood and university years there. Trabzon holds such a powerful place in my life. I read a biographical novel about Tamama whose life was affected by the exile [of Greek people from Turkey]. And I was very impressed. It was a life experience occurred in the places I knew very well. And it was a story about remembering. Or rather, it was a story about keeping secrets. The thing made me personally think was . . . This part is not detailed in the biography, but one of the things I concluded from it was that nobody was strong enough to keep a secret until they died. This is so powerful and harsh. We're not that strong. We eventually whisper it to someone. Like dying old people who happen to use a different language or suddenly reveal a secret or a sin. It is hard to die with your secret or sin, without a clean conscience. It is something as hard as stone. To be able to do it is a virtue because you are taking your bad conscience together with you while you are dying. I'm* *really impressed by this notion. It also makes us rethink what memory is. The impossibility to die with your memories and secrets . . . And making this movie [*Waiting for the Clouds*] in a place I know very well, a place I tried to escape from while I was there and then I wish to be buried in when I die. Trabzon has a really powerful impact on me. Returning there with Ayşe Eleni [the female protagonist of* Waiting for the Clouds*] was a powerful experience. I started going back to and traveling there in 2001. I'd never visited Trabzon again after university and after my father's death. So, returning there was a powerful, a very emotional and moving experience.* Pandora's Box *actually followed the similar themes as the previous movie. Memory, the modern world . . . It is again a story about memory, or loss of memory. An Alzheimer's disease story in a modern setting. I wished to come closer to Istanbul. I was intrigued by the idea of traveling in the western Black Sea. It was a nice discovery due to its proximity to Istanbul, the central Anatolia and the Küre Mountains. But the main theme of the movie is memory with a story about Alzheimer's. I need to experience something before starting to write a story about it. During the filming of* Pandora's Box, *we traveled a lot in old coal fields in Zonguldak [a city in the Black Sea region of Turkey]. There were enormous service stations with 300 to 1000 people working. Parking stations, or rather gas stations with outlets. There is a whole world in those places. When we were in one of those places, I met a young woman. And that was enough for me to start writing* Somewhere in Between. *We stopped there at 5 am on our way back from filming and everyone was minding their own business. But life is strange. An eye contact can change everything. We actually don't live in our own worlds all the time. The eye contact a young woman made with me while trying to complete her 24-hour shift led me to create an incredible story. It led me to strive to understand Zehra [the female protagonist of* Somewhere in Between*]. That eye contact was imprinted on my mind, impossible for me to forget. We filmed a very long therapy scene and edited it later. It was a process so intense that I felt like something was missing. We did what needed to be done, the editing was complete and enough. But I am still so impressed and I feel like I need to do something more about it. About a young woman who is lost in her own mind. I really want to understand that. I want to deal with the therapy scene again. I am actually not satisfied. Elmas [the protagonist of* Clair Obscur*] is born out of herself this way.*

Telling such stories in which the audience confronts the ghosts of the past and present is not so easy in a country like Turkey whose official policy is constructed on denial. What happens when a country cannot confront its past? The past might not pass but repeat itself in the present. Contemporary female filmmakers struggle for the past not to reappear. İpekçi's directorial story is a vivid example of such struggle. Pınar Fontini: *During the 1980 coup, your husband was imprisoned.*

Handan İpekçi: *Yes.*

Pınar Fontini: *And your first film is* "Dad is in the Army." *Is there a relationship between your film and your observations and experiences at that time?*

Handan İpekçi: *Of course. My husband was imprisoned for two and a half years. My child was also young at that time, they were born in 1978, and they were two and a half or three years old. During that period, I went to the prison regularly and had the opportunity to observe the children and their relatives. Of course, it was the children who impressed me the most. Because at that time, we, as adults, were experiencing the consequences of the path we chose, but the children did not have a choice, they were suffering the "punishment" of their parents' choices. Therefore, I observed those children and wanted to somehow reflect them in my film, and that's how* Dad is in the Army *came out.*

Pınar Fontini: *After that you made* Big Man, Little Love.

Handan İpekçi: *Yes. It might have been 1997, there were a lot of conflicts at that time, and soldiers were dying. The guerrillas who had gone to the mountains were dying and the Susurluk Scandal broke out. On the other hand, the 75th anniversary celebrations of the Turkish Republic were being held very enthusiastically. I actually thought like this: We are celebrating the 75th anniversary of the Republic, but Turkey is struggling with huge problems. I had to say something about this. It occurred to me to make a film about the Kurdish issue, which in my opinion is one of Turkey's biggest problems.*

It was Turkey's 75th anniversary at that time. And now the Turkish Republic is 101 years old. However, Kurdishness is still an issue. İpekçi had to deal with several problems after the release of *Big Man, Little Love*. Pınar Fontini: *The film also went abroad, but something happened there because of its name.*

Handan İpekçi: *The film's domestic title is* "Big Man Little Love" *and its international name is* "Big Man Little Love Hejar." *The name of the movie,* Hejar *[a Kurdish name], was found problematic. It was completely nonsensical. Then, the movie was inspected again five months later after it came out. This is also a first in the Turkish history, a movie inspected for the second time. Then, the movie was banned. I applied to the Council of State. The decision was in favor of the film. In fact, the film was about to complete its theatrical release, but after the banning attempt, 35,000 more people watched it. The film reached 135,000 viewers.*

İpekçi's struggle continued during the production of her third film *Hidden Faces*, which concentrates on violence towards women and honor killings. Pınar Fontini: *While you were making the film, there was a problem, an illness, right? One of your actors got sick and therefore the shooting was extended. And I think this has become a huge problem. Can you please talk a little bit about this?*

Handan İpekçi: *While filming, I figured out I wouldn't be able to finish the movie by December, 2005. I applied to the Ministry with my committee reports and asked for an extension to finish the movie. I pointed out the protagonist's illness constituted a force majeure, of course. They didn't accept it as a force majeure and they told me to deliver the film in December 2005. Of course I couldn't deliver it. The Ministry of Culture initiated the legal process, the support it gave was a low-interest loan, they turned it into legal interest and asked the tax office to collect the money. But of course, I was not sitting idle in the meantime, I was trying to finish the movie. The movie had scenes that needed to be shot in Istanbul and Germany, I was trying to shoot them. On the one hand, I was trying to find money, I was trying to find additional finance, on the other hand, I was trying to solve this problem with the Ministry of Culture. When they asked for the money back, I applied to the administrative court for the stay of execution. I lost the case. Then, I applied to the council of state. I lost the case again. 190,000 lira rose to 550,000 lira with the statutory interest. To solve the financial problem about* Hidden Faces, *I applied to the fund with* The Plane Tree. *So,* The Plane Tree *was a movie made to make money. Meanwhile, a tax amnesty was introduced. 550,000 lira was cut down and split into installments. It is a long story, which actually deserves its own movie. I paid the debt of this movie from 2011 to 2014, for three years. I am a female film director, I made a film about violence against women, I should be subjected to affirmative action. Because I touched upon a bleeding wound in society and made a film about it. I took responsibility but it felt like being punished which feels very heavy. So actually, as a female filmmaker, I felt like I was subjected to violence there, too. They made me experience this; it was a very bad feeling . . . I couldn't make movies in those years I could have been the most productive. It is painful, but I am not a victim. I will make movies as long as I live. I will continue making movies. Maybe I will make my most mature films in the future.*

As I explored in the first and last chapters of this book, Turkey feels impossible quite often. That is why we imagine a life somewhere away. Like me, like Mina [the female protagonist of *Present Tense*], like many other women, queer and Kurdish people living in Turkey. Söylemez went through similar emotions while making *Present Tense*.

Belmin Söylemez: *From the beginning, the movie was related to the experiences of mine and the young women I knew. What we had in mind was the stories of young women. I wanted to leave the country. So did my friends. Unemployment, lack of belonging, looking for a way out, not feeling that you really belong here were all among our themes. Also a young urban woman's quest for freedom, her desire to start all over again and leave everything behind. It had always been envisioned as the story of a young woman. And it ended up being so. Years passed, generations passed. But the desire to go has remained.*

Pınar Fontini: *Yes, it has. This is really important. The desire to go. We were so stuck. Istanbul was crushing up against all of us. The country was grinding us all down. It seemed to be impossible to go on like that. There was a general sense of misery. A sense of despair.* That is why I came to Melbourne. That is why Zeynep Dadak immigrated to Berlin. And Mizgin Müjde Arslan moved to London.

Mizgin Müjde Arslan: *That's actually one of the reasons why I moved to England, it was because I realized how limited I was [in Turkey]. After being detained . . . I think it was my most natural right, to go and ask these questions, it was a personal journey. And yet, even though I did not make a very political film [*I Flew You Stayed*], even though it was a family film, the attitude I encountered afterward was not a good attitude and it turned my sense of security upside down. This had an impact on me moving to the UK because I didn't feel safe in Turkey. I mean, I knew that as long as I was that man's daughter, as long as I was making these kinds of films, there would always be the sound of a police car or police radio on my neck, and I would be afraid that I might be detained at any moment. And I was going to make a movie with this fear . . . If you make a movie on this subject, you will be detained, you may go to prison, you will never be able to find a producer, you will not be able to find support, and you will not even be able to find people to work in your crew. I mean, no one will even come to shoot a movie with you. In order to liberate myself in every aspect . . . What do I really want to film, what is my problem as a woman, as a Middle Easterner? I came to England to see this better. In short, censorship covers us to a much greater extent than we think, we are not even aware of it. And I'm uncomfortable with that fear. After arriving [in the UK], I did not hear the sound of a police car or police radio for a long time. And after a few years, I realized that we constantly hear the alarm and siren sound in Turkey. The police are constantly coming to detain someone. This is a constant fear that they will raid a house and take us away. It really took me at least three years to get out of this state of fear, self-suppression, and censorship.*

Some of us decided to leave and some of us prefer/need to/have to stay. Pınar Fontini: *What is it like to be a creative woman or a female director in the Turkish film industry? What is your experience?*

Belmin Söylemez: *Difficult . . . It is very difficult, but on the other hand, I worked with someone like Bilge Olgaç [the fourth and most productive female filmmaker in Turkey], who came from the most difficult conditions and made her films easily and naturally under those conditions . . . In terms of how stories are told, women seem to be more fearless and free. Even when resources are tight, they push the limits and come up with stylistically distinct works.*

Zeynep Dadak: *Women carry the weight of the world on their shoulders! Of course, they can pull it off. Women can, of course, shoulder all kinds of projects, including the ones with a 100 million dollar budget. It is weird to discuss these things in terms of power or being powerful. Unfortunately, it is real. So, we need to keep resisting them while trying to find our language.*

Pınar Fontini: *Since both language and concepts are masculine, they underlie the concept of power. This does not mean that women are not strong, but if we as women could shape that concept of power in language, which we can and I think we are, then the power would point to something else and we would be strong and we already are.*

Zeynep Dadak: *Yes! We don't have to be strong either . . . This is something that is talked about within the whole Black Lives Matter and the Black movement that started and rose in America. I mean, how difficult it is for a Black woman to constantly try to present herself as strong, for example, to prove that she is not sensitive. On the contrary, because what gives that woman her strength is her sensitivity and vulnerability; if so. Again, as you said, what is coded as negative and what is positive is such a social process . . . If the language changes, what strength means, what weakness means, what sensitivity means will change. For example, it was not in vain that I studied arabesque during my doctorate. Men are the ones who cry the most, are the most sensitive, they are "the most," their pain is precious, worth telling. Or, if the woman's story is worth telling, she should be told through her victimization. Something terrible must have happened to her. Searching for something beyond this, giving the right to speak to people who have not experienced anything terrible . . . Because defining women based on the terrible things that have happened to them is also something that helps to reproduce the myths of victims and saviors. That's why I think questioning this language itself is a very important thing.*

This is the motivation that moves Dadak to make films on women who are neither victims nor heroines. As I also explored in the fourth chapter of this book, her film language is about not creating a catharsis. Rather than a person, she focuses on a group and shows us their moments of worry and joy without invoking extreme emotions. Pınar Fontini: *It is all a different language, isn't it? It is beyond what we are used to in cinema, away from the dominating codes. It is also not in opposition to them.*

Zeynep Dadak: *No, it is not.*

Pınar Fontini: *Can we say that it is a female language? Or is it inconvenient to describe it as such?*

Zeynep Dadak: *Jane Campion is one of my all-time favorite directors. She makes amazing cathartic dramas based on a conventional conflict as we know it. But she makes other kinds of films, as well. We shouldn't put them in opposition to each other. I got the chance to meet her years ago. I knew that she also studied anthropology. She even has a master's degree, so she used to write on the subject. But then, she quit. As someone who was on a similar path, I asked her how her academic past and filmmaking practices overlapped. Did they overlap at all? Or did she leave her academic past behind? She said, "Things you read, think or write about become the knowledge which creates and shapes you or defines your outlook on the world. They become something corporeal and sensual." It is favorable to describe a specific cinematic language as female within the patriarchal discourse. If a man writes a scenario, they say it is mathematical. If a woman writes a scenario, they say it is like a piece of lacework. We do not need those descriptions. But what shapes my outlook on the world is, of course, feminism. How could it not have affected it anyway?*

I investigated this particularity of women's cinema in the fifth chapter under the concept, "experiential filmmaking." As Dadak also mentions, things we read, think, or write about become the knowledge that shapes our outlook on the world and it is reflected in the work we do. Or as Esmer says, life experience is the source of filmmaking experience.

Pelin Esmer: *This is a bit of a natural life experience, life, getting to know each other, you predict who will react how and what they might say. You may also encounter something very surprising, after all, whatever comes your way is your luck. But I think the documentary director must have a very keen sense of smell and very good hearing because, with those sense organs, you are actually trying to catch a dilemma that is about to happen there. So, you have to sense that something is about to happen here, it may happen; so as to catch this, I should be ready for it. With the right question, maybe with the right angle . . . Because this is a momentary thing. After all, this is the most exciting and enjoyable part since there is no repetition. You need to be working all your sense organs at the highest level. These are really vital, worldly and very enjoyable emotions.*

Ustaoğlu explains this phenomenon by giving an example from her masterpiece, *Journey to The Sun*.

Yeşim Ustaoğlu: *After my short films, while I was writing* The Trace *and* Journey to The Sun, *I was already aware of the fact that writing was a complicated process. Writing is really insatiable. In order for you to be satisfied with your own movie, you have to know your characters closely and write them in depth. It is an adventure. If you want to tell an authentic story as dense as an experience with real people, that really touches the audience, you have to literally create Mehmet [the protagonist of* Journey to The Sun*]. It does not matter what Mehmet experiences. What matters is how he experiences it. How he feels. You really need to know Mehmet in order to tell how he feels. As a complete character, you should know Mehmet in every possible way. You do not have to show him in all aspects, but you should know him really well. In order to tell how he feels, you need to know his personality, his mood, his being, his state of mind, his socio-cultural identity, the space he lives in, all his social problems and worries. And how he internalizes or cannot internalize all of these. You should be able to define him as much as you can define yourself. We cannot always define ourselves easily. We have many weaknesses, dilemmas, worries, and problems. We need to understand them, as well. What are the character's weaknesses? After all, you are trying to create a person, a character. You are actually trying to find parallels with yourself during the writing process. Regardless of what kind of character you are writing. Regardless of the cultural identity or social class of the character, you are seeking parallels with yourself. If you are able to define yourself, you will be familiar with dilemmas, fears or weaknesses people may have in certain situations. You will know how a weakness defines you. While creating a character, you need to think of them as equally complicated.*

Ustaoğlu's description reminded me of one of the dreams John Berger saw in which he was the "dealer of appearances" (Berger 2020). He tells his dream as such:

> I had a dream in which I was a strange dealer: a dealer in looks or appearances. I collected and distributed them. In the dream I had just discovered a secret! I discovered it on my own, without help or advice. The secret was to get inside whatever I was looking at—a bucket of water, a cow, a city (like Toledo) seen from above, an oak tree; and once inside, to arrange its appearances for the better. *Better* did not mean making the thing seem more beautiful or more harmonious; nor did it mean making it more typical, so that the oak tree might represent all oak trees; it simply meant making it more itself so that the cow or the city or the bucket of water became more evidently unique! The *doing* of this gave me pleasure and I had the impression that the small changes I made from the inside, gave pleasure to others. The secret of how to get inside the object so as to rearrange how it looked was as simple as opening the door of a wardrobe. Perhaps it was merely a question of being there when the door swung open on its own. (Berger 2020; original emphasis)

Berger was entering inside the objects to make them look more like themselves. In Ustaoğlu's case, she seeps into herself to be able to create a unique character. Ustaoğlu does not depict female characters that are representative of all other women but what she does is simply make Zehra, Eleni, Elmas, or Şehnaz be representative more of their own uniqueness. It is her way of creating, or in Berger's terms, dealing with appearances.

Yeşim Ustaoğlu: *Since my very early inexperienced days, I've tried to build a perception, a cinematic and narrative style that focuses on human, time and space. Since my very early inexperienced days . . . It stems from my personality, my character, my being, my way of existence. What creates a story is our ways of existence. It leads us to say something. Trying to be like someone else . . . I mean, you can learn the technical stuff from someone else, from books and school. But your speech belongs to you. What comes out of my mouth is my speech, my style, my thinking and feeling mechanism. It only belongs to me. You can't learn it. It's a way of existence. It's my whole relation to life, to existing. It includes my experiences, my feelings, things I internalized or couldn't internalize, my impact and everything I've been impacted by. Things we internalized are not always positive. A way of existence is shaped by all kinds of positive and negative things. All these things correspond to what I do, the art I perform. My way of existence is always all about belonging. About perceiving, being on the road, existing and transforming on the road.*

That is how I understand people's ability to create. It just requires courage and freedom with which one confronts one's own self or it is merely a question of being curious to be there when the door opens on its own. All the filmmakers who contributed to the making of this project helped me to find these answers. These answers not only enabled me to write this book but also to realize a documentary project. I made my first film, *Dream Workers*, on the stories of these female directors (Figure E1). I would like to finish this section by revealing my own filmmaking journey[2] which is another story within Women's New Cinema.

On the eve of the global Covid-19 pandemic, I returned from Melbourne to Istanbul to begin filming the documentary. My initial plan for the production of the documentary was to record the interviews with the contemporary female directors at the Atlas Theatre in Istanbul and travel in Turkey to visit locations of the films made by the female filmmakers. A couple of days after I started the filmmaking process, the Cultural Ministry decided to close Atlas Theatre down to open a new theatre there. Welcoming this coincidence into the documentary, I decided to film the about-to-be-gentrified Atlas Theatre. I wanted to depict how my filmmaking process was affected by the cultural politics of the current government even before the production started. I started filming the closure of the theatre while searching for an alternative place for the interviews. This is when the pandemic broke out.

Figure E1 The poster of the documentary *Dream Workers*.

Instead of stopping production, I evaluated whatever I had in the house and started using this as my equipment—such as the projector, phones, and books as tripods. My friend Nalan Abbasoğlu turned into a cinematographer, and we learned how to use Filmic Pro, a 4K video recorder for mobile phones, from YouTube tutorials. Turning my living room into a studio, we filmed the live interviews with the female filmmakers that took place over Skype. They were projected onto the wall through the projector. When the curfews were announced, I started filming myself entrapped in the house. The film ended up reflecting the experience of making a film under the pandemic conditions.

I had completely different plans at first, but in the end, it turned out to be a much better film. That is why I think making a movie feels like flowing with the rhythm of life; when you open yourself to possibility and surprise, it can take you to a completely different place. Or as Simone Weil says, "That is what comes about when we know how to make every accomplished fact, whatever it may be, an object of desire" ([1951] 2021, 158–9). Like Agnès Varda does in her movie *The Gleaners and I* (2000). While talking to and working with potato gleaners, Varda finds some potatoes in the shape of a heart. She takes them home and lets them sprout and wrinkle. She then contrasts close-up views of the old spots on her hands with the wrinkles of decaying potatoes. That is how she opens her narrative for interpretation, by opening the narrative to life. Her caring gaze finding the heart-shaped potatoes might be a prescription for the art of film-making and the art of living a beautiful life.

List of Semi-structured Interviews

Date of Interview	Interviewee	Place
April 20, 2020	Arslan, Mizgin Müjde	Istanbul
May 10, 2020	İpekçi, Handan	Istanbul
May 25, 2020	Esmer, Pelin	Istanbul
June 11, 2020	Dadak, Zeynep	Istanbul
June 21, 2020	Söylemez, Belmin	Istanbul
June 28, 2020	Ustaoğlu, Yeşim	Istanbul

Notes

1. The extended version of this interview (with Mizgin Müjde Arslan) was published by *Studies in Documentary Film* (Fontini, 2024b), copyright Taylor & Francis, available online: https://doi.org/10.1080/17503280.2024.2425130.
2. The extended version of my own filmmaking journey was published by *Academic Quarter* (Fontini, 2024a), available online: https://doi.org/10.54337/academicquarter.i27.8828

Filmography

11'e 10 Kala / 10 to 11. Pelin Esmer, 2009, Turkey / France / Germany.
Adı Vasfiye / Her Name is Vasfiye. Atıf Yılmaz, 1985, Turkey.
Ah Gözel İstanbul / Invisible to the Eye. Zeynep Dadak, 2020, Turkey / Germany.
Ah. Merve Kayan, 2006, Turkey.
Anayurdu / Motherland. Senem Tüzen, 2015, Turkey / Greece.
Araf / Somewhere in Between. Yeşim Ustaoğlu, 2012, Turkey / France / Germany.
Atlıkarınca / Merry-Go-Round. İlksen Başarır, 2011, Turkey.
Aud. Merve Kayan, 2003, Turkey.
Ayna Ayna / Mirror Mirror. Belmin Söylemez, 2022, Turkey.
Babam Askerde / Dad is in the Army. Handan İpekçi, 1995, Turkey.
Bakur / North. Çayan Demirel and Ertuğrul Mavioğlu, 2015, Turkey.
Başka Dilde Aşk / Love in Another Language. İlksen Başarır, 2009, Turkey.
Ben ve Nuri Bala / Me and Nuri Bala. Melisa Önel, 2009, Turkey.
Benim Sinemalarım / My Cinemas. Füruzan and Karamustafa, 1990, Turkey.
Big Man Little Love, Hejar. Handan İpekçi, 2001, Turkey / Greece / Hungary.
Bir Avuç Deniz / A Handful of Sea. Leyla Yılmaz, 2011, Turkey.
Bir Varmış Bir Yokmuş. İlksen Başarır, 2015, Turkey.
Bitmeyen Yol / The Road That Has No End. Duygu Sağıroğlu, 1965, Turkey.
Bu Ne Güzel Demokrasi / What a Beautiful Democracy. Belmin Söylemez, Berke Baş, Somnur Vardar, Haşmet Topaloğlu, 2008, Turkey.
Bu Sahilde / On the Coast. Zeynep Dadak and Merve Kayan, 2010, Turkey.
Bulutları Beklerken / Waiting for the Clouds. Yeşim Ustaoğlu, 2003, Turkey / France / Germany / Greece.
Çalıştır Saksıyı. Zeynep Dadak, 2001, Turkey.
Çınar Ağacı / The Plane Tree. Handan İpekçi, 2011, Turkey.
Debt / Borç. Vuslat Saraçoğlu. 2018, Turkey.
Demsala dawi: Sewaxan/ The Last Season: Shawaks. Kazım Öz, 2009, Turkey.
Evcilik / Playing House. Bingöl Elmas, 2012, Turkey.
Ez Firiyam Tu Mayî Li Cî / I Flew You Stayed. Mizgin Müjde Arslan, 2012, Turkey.
Fakat Müzeyyen Bu Derin Bir Tutku. Çiğdem Vitrinel, 2014, Turkey.
Filmin Adı Ne? / What's the Name of the Film? Pınar Fontini, 2022, Turkey.
Gelin / The Bride. Ömer Lüdfi Akad, 1973, Turkey.

Geriye Kalan / What Remains. Çiğdem Vitrinel, 2012, Turkey.
Gidiş Geliş Gidiş. Zeynep Dadak, 2004, Turkey.
Gözetleme Kulesi / Watchtower. Pelin Esmer, 2012, Turkey / France / Germany.
Güneşe Yolculuk / Journey to The Sun. Yeşim Ustaoğlu, 1999, Turkey / Netherlands / Germany.
Gurbet Kuşları / Birds of Exile. Halit Refiğ, 1964, Turkey.
Hævnen / In a Better World. Susanne Bier, 2010, Denmark / Sweden.
Hay Way Zaman: Dersim'in Kayıp Kızları/Unburied in The Past—The Missing Girls of The Dersim. Nezahat Gündoğan, 2014, Turkey.
Hayaletler / Ghosts. Azra Deniz Okyay, 2020, Turkey / France / Qatar.
Hayatboyu / Lifelong. Aslı Özge, 2013, Turkey / Germany / Netherlands.
İki Tutam Saç: Dersim'in Kayıp Kızları / Two Locks of Hair: The Lost Girls of Dersim. Nezahat Gündoğan, 2010, Turkey.
İşe Yarar Bir Şey / Something Useful. Pelin Esmer, 2017, Turkey / France / Germany / Netherlands.
İz / The Trace. Yeşim Ustaoğlu, 1994, Turkey.
Jinen Dengbej / Women Dengbeji. Atölyemor Kolektifi, 2007, Turkey.
Kadınlar Cizre ve Silopi'yi Anlatıyor / Women Talk About Cizre and Silopi. Barış İçin Kadın Girişimi (Women for Women's Human Rights), 2015, Turkey.
Kanun Hükmü / The Decree. Nejla Demirci, 2023, Turkey.
Kaygı / Inflame. Ceylan Özgün Özçelik, 2017, Turkey.
Kemençenin Türküsü / Song of the Kemenche. Handan İpekçi, 1993, Turkey.
Kirasê Mirinê Hewîtî / A Fatal Dress: Polygamy, 2009, Turkey.
Köksüz / Nobody's Home. Deniz Akçay, 2014, Turkey.
Koleksiyoncu / The Collector. Pelin Esmer, 2022, Turkey.
Kraliçe Lear / Queen Lear. Pelin Esmer, 2019, Turkey.
Kumun Tadı / Seaburners. Melisa Önel, 2014, Turkey.
Kurak Günler / Burning Days. Emin Alper, 2022, Turkey / France / Germany / Netherlands / Greece / Croatia.
La battaglia di Algeri / The Battle of Algiers. Gillo Pontecorvo, 1966, Italy / Algeria.
La Hora de Los Hornos / The Hour of the Furnaces. Octavio Getino and Fernando E. Solanas, 1968, Argentina.
Les glaneurs et la glaneuse / The Gleaners and I. Agnès Varda, 2000, France.
Mamak'ta. Sezgin Türk, 2010, Turkey.
Mavi Dalga / The Blue Wave. Zeynep Dadak and Merve Kayan, 2013, Turkey / Netherlands / Greece / Germany.
Nahide'nin Türküsü / Hush! Berke Baş, 2009, Turkey.
Nefesim Kesilene Kadar / Until I Lose My Breath. Emine Emel Balcı, 2015, Turkey / Germany.
Onun Filmi / Her First. Su Baloğlu and Merve Bozcu, 2019, Turkey.
Oyun / The Play. Pelin Esmer, 2005, Turkey.
Pandora'nın Kutusu / Pandora's Box. Yeşim Ustaoğlu, 2008, Turkey / France / Germany / Belgium.
Peri Tozu. Ela Alyamaç, 2008, Turkey.
Pippa'ya Mektubum / My Letter to Pippa. Bingöl Elmas, 2010, Turkey / France.

Qiblenameya Deya Min / My Mother's Compass. Hatice Kamer, 2013, Turkey.
Réponses de femmes: Notre corps, notre sexe / Women Reply: Our Bodies, Our Sex. Agnès Varda, 1975, France.
Saklı Yüzler / Hidden Faces. Handan İpekçi, 2007, Turkey.
Seni Seviyorum Rosa / Rosa, I Love You. Özgentürk, 1992, Turkey / Greece / France / Switzerland.
Senin Yıllardır Gerçekleştirmeyi Beklediğin Bir Düş Var / Dream Workers. Pınar Fontini, 2022, Turkey.
Şimdiki Zaman / Present Tense. Belmin Söylemez, 2012, Turkey.
Sırtlarındaki Hayat / Life on Their Shoulders. Yeşim Ustaoğlu, 2004, Turkey / France.
Sweet Splits. Merve Kayan and Mierle Laderman Ukeles, 2005, Turkey.
Takhté siah / Blackboards. Samira Makhmalbaf, 2000, Iran / Italy / Japan.
Tarihe Şerh: Irak Dünya Mahkemesi. Zeynep Dadak, 2007, Turkey.
Tereddüt / Clair Obscur. Yeşim Ustaoğlu, 2016, Turkey / France / Germany / Poland.
The Gift. Merve Kayan, 2003, Turkey.
Toz Bezi / Dust Cloth. Ahu Öztürk, 2015, Turkey / Germany.
Vesikalı Yarim / My Prostitute Love. Ömer Lüdfi Akad, 1968, Turkey.
Work. Merve Kayan, 2008, Turkey.
Zefir / *Zephyr*. Bellmen Baş, 2010, Turkey.
Zer. Kazım Öz, 2017, Germany / Turkey / United States.

References

Abisel, Nilgün. 1994. *Türk Sineması Üzerine Yazılar*. Ankara: İmge Yayınevi.

Ahmed, Sara. 2010. *The Promise of Happiness*. Durham and London: Duke University Press.

Ahmed, Sara. 2016. "An Affinity of Hammers." *TSQ: Transgender Studies Quarterly* 3 (1–2): 22–34. https://doi.org/10.1215/23289252-3334151.

Ahmed, Sara. 2017a. "Kessler Lecture 'Queer Use.'" In *CLAGS: The Center for LGBTQ Studies*. https://www.youtube.com/watch?v=O8Y_P27vVAQ.

Ahmed, Sara. 2017b. *Living a Feminist Life*. Durham and London: Duke University Press.

Ahmed, Sara. 2021. "Complaint as Feminist Pedagogy." 2021. https://feministkilljoys.com/2021/06/16/complaint-as-feminist-pedagogy/.

Ahmed, Sara. 2023. *The Feminist Killjoy Handbook*. Penguin Books.

Aidoo, Ama Ata. 1994. *Our Sister Killjoy*. Longman.

Akça, Kerem. 2018. "No Title." 2018. https://twitter.com/kerem_akca?lang=en.

Akkaya, Ercan. 2016. "Rethinking Independent Cinema : Public Funding, Market Oligopoly and the Film Industry in Turkey." Bogazici University. https://doi.org/10.13140/RG.2.2.27329.97124.

Akser, Murat, and Deniz Bayrakdar, eds. 2014. *New Cinema, New Media: Reinventing Turkish Cinema*. Newcastle upon Tyne: Cambridge Scholars Publishing.

Algan, Necla. 2010. "Üç Yönetmenden Taşra Görünümleri." In *Taşrada Var Bir Zaman*, edited by Zeynep Tül Akbal Süalp and Aslı Güneş. İstanbul: Çitlembik.

Alkan, Hülya. 2014. "Spatial Realism: From Urban to Rural." In *New Cinema, New Media: Reinventing Turkish Cinema*. Newcastle upon Tyne: Cambridge Scholars Publishing.

Althusser, Louis. 2006. *İdeoloji ve Devletin İdeolojik Aygıtları*. İstanbul: İthaki.

Altyazı Fasikül. 2023. "10 Başlıkta 2023: Sinemada 'Özgürlük.'" *Altyazı Fasikül: Özgür Sinema*. 2023.

Anzaldua, Gloria. 1987. *Borderlands/La Frontera: The New Mestiza*. San Francisco: Aunt Lute Press.

Arslan, Savaş. 2011. *Cinema in Turkey: A New Critical History*. New York: Oxford University Press. https://doi.org/10.1093/screen/hjr043.

Arslan, Umut Tümay. 2015. "Türklük Ethosu ve Suçluluk Sorunu." Azad Alik. 2015. https://azadalik.wordpress.com/2015/10/02/turkluk-ethosu-ve-sucluluk-sorunu-mesele-dergisinde-19151/.

Arslan, Umut Tümay. 2019. *Kat Sinema ve Etik*. İstanbul: Metis Yayınları.

Arslan, Umut Tümay. 2021. "Kendini Hesaba Katmak: Tanıklık ve Meçhul Olan." *5 Harfliler*, May 2021. https://www.5harfliler.com/kendini-hesaba-katmak/.

Arslan, Umut Tümay. 2022a. "Türklük Ethosu ve Kürtler." *Özgür Politika*, February 2022.

Arslan, Umut Tümay. 2022b. "Eril Bakış—Umut Tümay Arslan (Feminist Bellek)." *Sendika.Org*, March 2, 2022.

Arslan, Umut Tümay. 2022c. "Kadınların Sineması: Efendinin Bakışı Efendinin Perdesini Asla Yırtmaz." *5 Harfliler*, December 2022.

Asmin Film. 2010. "Pippa'ya Mektubum Filminin Festival Yolculuğu Deavm Ediyor." 2010.

Atakav, Eylem. 2013. *Women and Turkish Cinema: Gender Politics, Cultural Identity and Representation*. New York: Routledge. https://doi.org/10.4324/9780203810378.

Atasoy, Orhan. 1992. "Orhan Atasoy - Gemiler." 1992.

Aydemir, Şenay, Evrim Kaya, Fırat Yücel, and Kaan Müjdeci. 2016. *Kapalı Gişe: Türkiye'de Tekelleşen Film Dağıtımı [Only Blockbusters Left Alive]*. Turkey.

Aydemir, Vedat. 2017. "Zer Filmi, Ilk Gösteriminde Sansüre Uğradı." *Evrensel*, April 12, 2017. https://www.evrensel.net/haber/315597/zer-filmi-ilk-gosteriminde-sansure-ugradi.

Aytaç, Senem, and Ayça Çiftçi. 2017. "Bir Kadın Hatırladı." *Altyazı*, May 2017.

Aytaç, Senem, and Berke Göl. 2012. "Çiğdem Vitrinel: Kaybedilen Bir Oyunu Sürdürmek." *Altyazı*, no. 120: 38–40.

Barış, Janet. 2010. "Kentin Taşralaşmasıyla İç İçe Geçen Haller." In *Taşrada Var Bir Zaman*, edited by Zeynep Tül Akbal Süalp and Aslı Güneş, 279–89. İstanbul: Çitlembik.

Bell, Jeffrey. 1997. "Thinking with Cinema: Deleuze and Film Theory." *Film-Philosophy* 1 (1): null. https://doi.org/10.3366/film.1997.0008.

Benhabib, Seyla. 2013. "Turkey's Authoritarian Turn." *New York Times*. 2013. https://www.nytimes.com/2013/06/04/opinion/turkeys-authoritarian-turn.html.

Berger, John. 2020. *Steps Towards a Small Theory of the Visible*. Penguin.

Berghahn, D, and C Sternberg. 2010. *European Cinema in Motion: Migrant and Diasporic Film in Contemporary Europe*. Palgrave European Film and Media Studies. New York: Palgrave Macmillan UK. https://books.google.com.tr/books?id=d3xaCwAAQBAJ.

Berlinale Talents. 2017. "Ceylan Özgün Özçelik, Senem Aytaç | 'Between the Lines: Film, Critique.'" Germany. https://www.youtube.com/watch?v=mVUBNbGzSJg.

Bianet. 2022. "Bakanlık 'Kurak Günler'e Verdiği Desteği Faiziyle Geri Istedi," December 8, 2022. https://bianet.org/haber/bakanlik-kurak-gunler-e-verdigi-destegi-faiziyle-geri-istedi-271127.

Bilal, Melisa, and Lerna Ekmekçioğlu. 2006. *Bir Adalet Feryadı Osmanlı'dan Türkiye'ye Beş Ermeni Feminist Yazar*. İstanbul: Aras.

Black, Angie, Patrick Kelly, Kim Munro, and Stayci Taylor. 2023. "A Mani-Pedi-Anti-Counter-FESTO for Queer Screen Production Practice (film)." https://revistas.ucp.pt/index.php/jsta/article/view/11736. https://doi.org/10.26188/25845841

Blonski, Annette, Barbara Creed, and Freda Freiberg, eds. 1987. *Don't Shoot Darling, Women's Independent Filmmaking in Australia*. Richmond, Australia: Greenhouse Publications Pty Ltd.

Bolsom, Erika. 2018. "'There Is No Such Thing as Documentary': An Interview with Trinh T. Minh-Ha." *Frieze*, November 2018.

Bora, Tanıl. 2007. "Türkiye'de Siyasal İdeolojilerde ABD/Amerika İmgesi." In *Modernleşme ve Batıcılık*, 147–69. İstanbul: İletişim Yayınları.

Bordwell, David, Janet Staiger, and Kristin Thompson. 1985. *The Classical Hollywood Cinema: Film Style and Mode of Production to 1960*. New York: Columbia University Press.

Bovenschen, Silvia. 1977. "Is There a Feminine Aesthetic?" *New German Critique* 10.

Bruno, Giuliana. 2018. *Atlas of Emotion Journeys in Art, Architecture, and Film*. New York: New Left Books.

Büker, Seçil. 2002. "The Film Does Not End With an Ecstatic Kiss." In *Fragments of Culture: The Everyday of Modern Turkey*, edited by Deniz Kandiyoti and Ayşe Saktanber. London: Tauris.

Bulley, Victoria Adukwei. 2020. "Interview with Saidiya Hartman." *The White Review*. 2020.

Butler, Alison. 2002. *Women's Cinema: The Contested Screen*. London: Wallflower Press.

Butler, Judith. 1997. *The Psychic Life of Power: Theories in Subjection*. CA: Stanford University Press.

Canaan, Andrea. 1981. "Brownness." In *This Bridge Called My Back: Writings by Radical Women of Color*, edited by Cherríe Moraga and Gloria Anzaldúa, 232–8. New York: Kitchen Table: Women of Color Press.

Carlson, Bronwyn, and Ryan Frazer. 2021. "Futures." In: *Indigenous Digital Life*. Cham: Palgrave Macmillan.

Chaudhuri, Shohini, and Howard Finn. 2003. "The Open Image: Poetic Realism and the New Iranian Cinema." *Screen* 44 (1): 38–57. https://doi.org/10.1093/screen/44.1.38.

Çiçekoğlu, Feride. 2007. *Vesikalı Şehir*. Metis Yayınları.

Çiçekoğlu, Feride. 2015. *Şehrin İtirazı Gezi Direnişi Öncesi İstanbul Filmlerinde İsyan Eşiği*. İstanbul: Metis Yayınları.

Çiftçi, Ayça. 2009. "Kazım Öz Sineması: Konuşmak, Hatırlamak." In *Kürt Sineması: Yurtsuzluk, Sınır ve Ölüm*, 267–87. İstanbul: Agora Kitaplığı.

Citron, Michelle. 1999. "Fleeing from Documentary: Autobiographical Film/Video and the 'Ethics of Responsibility.'" In *Feminism and Documentary*, edited by Diane Waldman and Janet Walker, 271–86. Minneapolis and London: University of Minnesota Press.

Dadak, Zeynep, and Merve Kayan. 2014. "Zeyndep Dadak and Merve Kayan Taşra İllaki Minimalizm Bahanesi Mi Olacak?" *Xoxo Digital*, 2014.

Deleuze, Gilles, and Claire Parnet. 1990. *Diyaloglar*. Ankara: Bağlam.

Dink, Hrant. 2005. "New Sentences of Armenian Identity or When You Find the Water Crack. . ." In *İmparatorluğun Çöküş Döneminde Osmanlı Ermenileri: Bilimsel Sorumluluk ve Demokrasi Sorunları*. İstanbul: Bilgi Universitesi.

Dink, Rakel. 2017. "Rakel Dink: Gelin, bu ülkedeki güvercin tedirginliğini kaldıralım." *Agos* Newspaper, 2017.

Dönmez-Colin, Gönül. 2008. *Turkish Cinema: Identity, Distance, Belonging*. London: Reaktion Books.

Dönmez-Colin, Gönül. 2010. "Women in Turkish Cinema: Their Presence and Absence as Images and as Image-Makers." *Third Text* 24 (1): 91–105. https://doi.org/10.1080/09528820903488976.

Duran, Burhanettin. 2008. "The Justice and Development Party's 'New Politics': Steering toward Conservative Democracy, a Revised Islamic Agenda or Management of New Crises?" In *Secular and Islamic Politics in Turkey: The Making of the Justice and Development Party*, 80–106. Abingdon: Routledge.

D W Turkey. 2021. "Azra Deniz Okyay: Kadın Yönetmen Olduğum Için Elimden Işim Çok Alındı." 2021. https://www.dw.com/tr/azra-deniz-okyay-kadın-yönetmen-olduğum-için-elimden-işim-çok-alındı/video-56784474.

Elkin, Lauren. 2017. *Flaneuse: Women Walk the City in Paris, New York, Tokyo, Venice, and London*. New York: Farrar, Straus and Giroux.

Erdem, Tuna. 2019. "Savrulanı Saklamaya Çalışmak." *T24*, March 7, 2019. https://t24.com.tr/k24/yazi/savrulani-saklamaya-calismak,2180.

Erdoğan, Melek Şimşek. 2019. "2000'li Yıllarda Türkiye Sinemasında Taşranın Temsili." Ankara: Ankara University.

Erkılıç, Hakan. 2003. "Türk Sinemasının Ekonomik Yapısı ve Bu Yapının Sinemamıza Etkileri." İstanbul: Mimar Sinan Fine Arts University.

Ersoy, Bilal. 2019. "Psychology and Social Identity." In *Authoritarianism and Resistance in Turkey: Conversations on Democratic and Social Challenges*, edited by Esra Özyürek, Gaye Özpınar, and Emrah Altındiş. Switzerland: Springer.

Fischer, Lucy. 1989. *Shot/Countershot: Film Tradition and Women's Cinema*. Basingstoke and London: Macmillan and British Film Institute.

Flitterman-Lewis, Sandy. 1990. *To Desire Differently: Feminism and the French Cinema*. Urbana and Chicago: University of Illinois Press.

Fontini, Pinar. 2017. "1990–2000 Yılları Arasında Türkiye'de Kadın Yönetmen Olmak." İstanbul: Marmara University.

Fontini, Pinar. 2020. "Dert Bende Derman Sende Dert Bende Derman Bende: Türkiye Sineması Kadın Temsiline 'Arabesk' Bir Bakış." In *Arabesk Yeniden*, 149–62. İstanbul: Notabene.

Fontini, Pinar. 2022a. "Meet Me in the Evening for a Kiss in Taksim Square." *Feminist Review* 131 (1).

Fontini, Pinar. 2022b. "Her Resistance Is Many: The Accented Filmmaking Practice of Mizgin Müjde Arslan." *Feminist Media Studies* 23 (5): 2269–85.

Fontini, Pinar. 2024a. "On Academic Filmmaking as a 'Messy' Methodology." *Academic Quarter | Akademisk Kvarter*, nr. 27 (August): 71-82. https://doi.org/10.54337/academicquarter.i27.8828.

Fontini, Pinar. 2024b. "Mizgin Müjde Arslan and Women's Autobiographical Filmmaking." *Studies in Documentary Film*. http://dx.doi.org/10.1080/17503280.2024.2425130.

Foundation, Hrant Dink. 2007. "23.5 Hrant Dink Site of Memory." 2007. https://hrantdink.org/en/site-of-memory/about-23-5/story.

Franklin, Sarah. 2017. "Kessler Lecture 2017 Sara Ahmed." 2017. https://www.youtube.com/watch?v=O8Y_P27vVAQ&list=PLoFyAGi1tGr6XSCCEqAhN4pPKKjyjUx_2&index=3&t=877s.

Freud, Sigmund. 1919. "The 'Uncanny.'" *Sammlung, Fünfte Folge*.

Fromm, Erich. 1956. *The Art of Loving*. New York: Harper and Row. https://doi.org/10.2143/sis.5.0.2004163.

Frye, Marilyn. 1991. "Introduction." In *Are You Girls Traveling Alone? Adventures in Lesbianic Logic*, edited by Marilyn Murphy, 11–16. Los Angeles: Clothes Spin Fever.

Gabriel, Teshome. 1990. "Thoughts on Nomadic Aesthetics and the Black Independent Cinema: Traces of a Journey." In *Out There: Marginalization and Contemporary Cultures*, edited by Russell Ferguson, Martha Gever, Trinh T. Minh-ha, and Cornel West, 395–411. New York: New Museum of Contemporary Art.

Geçgin, Ayhan. 2018. *Gençlik Düşü*. İstanbul: Metis Yayınları.

Gledhill, Christine. 1999. "Pleasurable Negotiations." In *Feminist Film Theory: A Reader*. Edinburgh: Edinburgh University Press.

Godmilow, Jill. 2022. *Kill the Documentary: A Letter to Filmmakers, Students, and Scholars*. New York: Columbia University Press.

Grgic, Ana. 2017. "Kazım Öz on Zer." *East European Film Bulletin*, November 2017. https://eefb.org/interviews/kazim-oz-on-zer/.

Guin, Ursula K. Le. 1975. "Aussiecon (1975) Worldcon Ursula K. Le Guin Guest of Honor Speech." 1975. https://www.youtube.com/watch?v=Deuas-AuzbU.

Güngören, Didem Nur. 2014. "Mahremiyetler ve Masumiyetler." 5Harfliler. 2014. https://www.5harfliler.com/mahremiyetler-ve-masumiyetler/.

Gürbilek, Nurdan. 2001. *Vitrin'de Yaşamak 1980'lerin Kültürel İklimi*. İstanbul: Metis Yayınları.

Gürbilek, Nurdan. 2012. *Kötü Çocuk Türk*. İstanbul: Metis Yayınları.

Gürbilek, Nurdan. 2015. *Sessizin Payı*. İstanbul: Metis Yayınları.

Gürbilek, Nurdan. 2019. *Ev Ödevi*. İstanbul: Metis Yayınları.

Gürbilek, Nurdan. 2020. *İkinci Hayat: Kaçmak, Kovulmak, Dönmek Üzerine Denemeler*. İstanbul: Metis Yayınları.

Hall, Stuart. 1992. "Encoding, Decoding." In *Culture, Media, Language: Working Papers in Cultural Studies*, edited by Stuart Hall, Dorothy Hobson, Andrew Lowe, and Paul Willis. London: Routledge.

Hall, Stuart. 2017. *Temsil Kültürel Temsiller ve Anlamlandırma Uygulamaları*. İstanbul: Pinhan Yayıncılık.

Haraway, Donna. 1988. "Situated Knowledges: The Science Question in Feminism and the Privilege of Partial Perspective." *Feminist Studies* 14 (3): 575–99. https://doi.org/10.2307/3178066.

Hartman, Saidiya. 2020. *Wayward Lives Beautiful Experiments*. W. W. Norton and Company.

Higbee, Will, and Song Hwee Lim. 2010. "Concepts of Transnational Cinema: Towards a Critical Transnationalism in Film Studies." *Transnational Cinemas* 1 (1): 7–21. https://doi.org/10.1386/trac.1.1.7/1.

hooks, bell. 1990. "Marginality as a Site of Resistance." In *Out There: Marginalization and Contemporary Cultures*, edited by Russell Ferguson, Martha Gever, Trinh T. Minh-ha, and Cornel West, 341–3. New York: MIT Press, New Museum of Contemporary Art; Cambridge, MA.

hooks, bell. 1991. "Theory as Liberatory Practice." *Yale Journal of Law and Feminism* 1 (1).

hooks, bell. 1992. *Black Looks: Race and Representation*. New York: Routledge.

İlkkaracan, Pınar. 2017. "An Analysis of the 'Conservative Democracy' of the Justice and Development Party in Turkey." In *Sexual Politics in Muslim Societies*, edited by Pınar İlkkaracan and Rima Athar, 62–87. Jawa Timur: GAYa NUSANTARA & CSBR.

İnceoğlu, İrem. 2015. "Beyaz Perdede Kadın Anlatısı: Mavi Dalga Filminin Feminist İncelemesi." *Fe Dergi: Feminist Eleştiri Cilt*, no. 2: 87–93. https://doi.org/10.1501/Fe0001.

International Coalition for Filmmakers at Risk. 2022. "Release Çiğdem Mater!," April 28, 2022.

Irigaray, Luce. 2006. *Ben Sen Biz Farklılık Kültürüne Doğru*. Ankara: İmge Yayınevi.

Johnston, Claire. 1973. "Women's Cinema as Counter-Cinema." In *Notes on Women's Cinema*, 24–31. London: Society for Education in Film and Television.

Johnston, Claire. 1999. "Women's Cinema as Counter-Cinema." In *Feminist Film Theory A Reader*, edited by Sue Thornham, 31–40. Edinburgh: Edinburgh University Press.

Kanzler, Martin. 2014. "The Turkish Film Industry Key Developments 2004 to 2013." *European Audiovisual Observatory*, no. October.

Kaplan, Caren, and Inderpal Grewal. 1999. "Transnational Feminist Cultural Studies: Beyond the Marxism/Poststructuralism/Feminism Divides." In *Between Woman and Nation: Nationalism, Transnational Feminisms and the State*, edited by Caren Kaplan, Norma Alarcon, and Minao Moallem. Durham, NC: Duke University Press.

Keating, AnaLouise. 2013. "Beyond Intersectionality: Theorizing Interconnectivity with/in this Bridge Called My Back: Writings by Radical Women of Color." In *Transformation Now!: Toward a Post-Oppositional Politics of Change*, 29–60. Urbana, Chicago, and Springfield: University of Illinois Press. https://doi.org/10.5860/choice.51-7047.

Kelly, Gabrielle, and Cherly Robson, eds. 2014. *Celluloid Ceiling: Women Film Directors Breaking Through*. UK: Supernova Books.

Kırel, Serpil. 2004. "Kendi Evinde Misafir: Evsizleşen Ulusal Sinemalara Bir Örnek Olarak Türk Sineması." *Kültürel Üretim Alanları: Renkli Atlas. Nurçay Türkoğlu*, 99–124.

Kırel, Serpil. 2009. "Pelin Esmer'in 'Oyun' Belgeseli Çerçevesinde Kadın Deneyimlerinin Aktarılmasında Belgesel Filmin Yeri." *Culture and Communication* 12 (1): 127–59.

Knight, Julia. 1992. *Women and the New German Cinema*. London and New York: Verso.

Kobena, Mercer. 1994. "Diasporic Culture and the Dialogic Imagination: The Aesthetics of Black Independent Film in Britain." In *Welcome to the Jungle: New Positions in Black Cultural Studies*. New York: Routledge.

Koçer, Sinem. 2016. "Ez Firiyam Tu Mayî Li Cih (I Flew You Stayed / Ben Uçtum Sen Kaldın): An Example of Domestic Ethnography." In *Kurdish Documentary Cinema in Turkey: The Politics and Aesthetics of Identity and Resistance*, edited by Sinem Koçer and Can Candan, 131–40. Newcastle upon Tyne: Cambridge Scholars Publishing.

Köker, Eser. 1994. "Türk Filmlerinde Kadın ve Demokrasi İlişkisi." In *Türk Sinemasında Demokrasi Kavramının Gelişmesi*, 133–67. Ankara: T. C. Kültür Bakanlığı Milli Kütüphane Basımevi.

Kristeva, Julia. 1981. "Women's Time." *Signs* 7 (1): 13–35.

Kristeva, Julia. 1991. *Strangers to Ourselves*. New York: Columbia University Press.

Kuhn, Annette. 1994. *Women's Pictures Feminism and Cinema*. Manchester: Verso.

Kültür ve Turizm Bakanlığı Teftiş Kurulu Başkanlığı. 1986. "Sinema, Video ve Müzik Eserlerinin Denetlenmesi Hakkında Yönetmelik." 1986. https://teftis.ktb.gov.tr/TR-264591/sinemavideo-ve-muzik-eserlerinin-denetlenmesi-hakkinda-yonetmelik.html.

Kürkçü, Ertuğrul. 2014. "Velev Ki 90'lara Döndünüz. . ." Bianet. 2014. https://m.bianet.org/bianet/insan-haklari/161199-velev-ki-90-lara-dondunuz?fbclid=IwAR1BQAUyAKlJbLBQWF5CK9N7x5HQcykxcevdFb8njusm-adFRnNAKUWGv6Q.

Laing, Ronald David. 1971. *The Politics of the Family*. Middlesex: Penguin Books.
Lauretis, Teresa De. 1984. *Alice Doesn't: Feminism, Semiotics, Cinema*. London: MacMillan.
Lauretis, Teresa De. 1990a. "'Guerrilla in the Midst: Women's Cinema in the 80s.'" *Screen* 31 (1): 6–25.
Lauretis, Teresa De. 1990b. "Eccentric Subjects: Feminist Theory and Historical Consciousness." *Feminist Studies* 16 (1): 115–50.
Lauretis, Teresa De. 2007. "Rethinking Women's Cinema." In *Figures of Resistance Essays in Feminist Theory*, edited by Patricia White, 25–47. Urbana and Chicago: University of Illinois Press. https://doi.org/10.1215/9780822381723.
Lazreg, Marnia. 2000. "The Triumphant Discourse of Global Feminism: Should Other Women Be Known?" In *The Transnational Reception of Third World Women Writers*, edited by Amal Amireh and Lisa Suhair Majaj. New York: Garland Publishing.
Lorde, Audre. 1984a. "Poetry Is Not a Luxury." In *Sister Outsider*, 36–9. New York: Crossing Press.
Lorde, Audre. 1984b. "The Master's Tools Will Never Dismantle the Master's House." In *Sister Outsider*, 110–13. New York: Crossing Press.
Lorde, Audre. 2007. *Sister Outsider*. New York: Ten Speed Press.
Lorde, Audre. 2017a. *A Burst of Light and Other Essays*. Mineola, New York: Ixia Press.
Lorde, Audre. 2017b. *Your Silence Will Not Protect You*. UK: Silver Press.
Lorde, Audre, and James Baldwin. 1984. "Revolutionary Hope: A Conversation Between James Baldwin and Audre Lorde." *Essence Magazine*. 1984.
Loshitzky, Y. 2010. *Screening Strangers: Migration and Diaspora in Contemporary European Cinema*. New Directions in National Cinemas. Bloomington: Indiana University Press. https://books.google.com.tr/books?id=ELJRN4mNGiIC.
Luxembourgeus, Tage T. E., and Mumin Baris, eds. 2018. *The New Wave in Turkey's Cinema*. Proverbial Elephant.
Marks, Laura. 1994. "A Deleuzian Politics of Hybrid Cinema." *Screen*, no. 3: 244–64.
Marks, Laura U. 2000. *The Skin of Film: Intercultural Cinema, Embodiment, and the Senses*. Durham, NC, and London: Duke University Press.
Mayne, Judith. 1990. *The Woman at the Keyhole: Feminism and Women's Cinema*. Bloomington and Indianapolis: Indiana University Press.
McKittrick, Katherine. 2021. "Curiosities (My Heart Makes My Head Swim)." In *Dear Science and Other Stories*, 2: 1–13. Durham, NC: Duke University Press. https://doi.org/10.1515/9781478012573.
Mehra, Nishta J. 2017. "Sara Ahmed: Notes from a Feminist Killjoy." *Guernica*. 2017.
Mellencamp, Patricia. 1995. *A Fine Romance: Five Ages of Film Feminism*. Philadelphia: Temple University Press.
Minh-ha, Trinh T. 1991. *When The Moon Waxes Red*. New York: Routledge.
Modleski, Tania. 1999. *Old Wives' Tales: Feminist Re-Visions of Film and Other Fictions*. London and New York: I. B. Tauris.
Mohanty, Chandra Talpade. 1991a. "Cartographies of Struggle: Third World Women and the Politics of Feminism." In *Third World Women and The Politics of Feminism*, edited by Chandra Talpade Mohanty, Ann Russo, and Lourdes Torres, 1–50. Bloomington and Indianapolis: Indiana University Press.

Mohanty, Chandra Talpade. 1991b. "Under Western Eyes: Feminist Scholarship and Colonial Discourses." In *Third World Women and The Politics of Feminism*, edited by Chandra Talpade Mohanty, Ann Russo, and Lourdes Torres, 51–80. Bloomington and Indianapolis: Indiana University Press.

Morales, Rosario. 1981. "We're All in the Same Boat." In *This Bridge Called My Back: Writings by Radical Women of Color*, edited by Cherríe Moraga and Gloria Anzaldúa, 91–3. New York: Kitchen Table: Women of Color Press.

Morrison, Toni. 1998. *The Bluest Eye*. New York: Vintage Books.

Moten, Fred. 2017. *Black and Blur*. Durham, NC, and London: Duke University Press.

Moyers, Bill. 1990. "Toni Morrison on Love and Writing." 1990.

Mulvey, Laura. 1999. "Visual Pleasure and Narrative Cinema." In *Feminist Film Theory: A Reader*, edited by Sue Thornham, 58–69. Edinburgh: Edinburgh University Press.

Munk, Yael. 2011. "Ethics and Responsibility: The Feminization of the New Israeli Documentary." *Israel Studies* 16 (2): 151–64. https://doi.org/10.1080/14660466.2019.1654357.

Naficy, Hamid. 2001. *An Accented Cinema: Exilic and Diasporic Filmmaking*. Princeton: Princeton University Press.

Neyzi, Leyla. 2013. *"Ben Kimim?" Türkiye'de Sözlü Tarih, Kimlik ve Öznellik*. İstanbul: İletişim Yayınları.

Nichols, Bill. 1991. *Representing Reality: Issues and Concepts in Documentary*. Bloomington: Indiana University Press.

O'Sullivan, Sandy. 2023. "Trans Art, Archives and Creative Practices: A Collective Conversation." In University of Melbourne's Faculty of Arts, Diversity and Inclusion, and the Gender Studies Program.

Oğur, Erkan, and Djivan Gasparyan. 2013. "Erkan Oğur and Djivan Gasparyan – Zahit Bizi Tan Eyleme." Kalan Müzik. 2013.

Orta, Nermin. 2012. "Gemiden ve Laleli'de Bir Azize: 90'larla Gelen Yeni Sinemacılar." In *Her Şeye Rağmen Ayakta – 90'lı Yıllar Türkiye Sineması*, edited by Şükran Kuyucak Esen, 172–87. AKSAV.

Ottone, Giovanni. 2017. *New Cinema in Turkey: Filmmakers and Identities between Urban and Rural Space*. Newcastle upon Tyne: Cambridge Scholars Publishing.

Özbudun, Ergun. 2006. "From Political Islam to Conservative Democracy: The Case of the Justice and Development Party in Turkey." *South European Society and Politics* 11: 543–57.

Özgüç, Agah. 1988. *Türk Sinemasında Cinselliğin Tarihi*. İstanbul: Broy Yayınları.

Özgüç, Agah. 1993. *100 Filmde Başlangıcından Günümüze Türk Sineması*. Ankara: Bilgi Yayınevi.

Özlü, Tezer. 1994. "Ev." In *Çocukluğun Soğuk Geceleri*, 7–17. İstanbul: Yapı Kredi Yayınları.

Öztürk, S. Ruken. 2004. *Sinemanın "Dişil" Yüzü Türkiye'de Kadın Yönetmenler*. İstanbul: Om Yayınevi.

Öztürk, S Ruken. 2010. "Hard to Bear: Women's Burdens in the Cinema of Yeşim Ustaoğlu." In *Visions of Struggle in Women's Filmmaking in the Mediterranean*, edited by Flavia Laviosa, 149–64. New York: Palgrave Macmillan.

Öztürk, S. Ruken, and Nilgün Tutal. 2001. "Sinemada Kadın Karakterin Sessizliği: Sessizlik Bir Direnme Pratiği Olabilir Mi?" *İetişim* 10: 101–26.

Parla, Jale. 2019. "Turkish Literature." In *Authoritarianism and Resistance in Turkey: Conversations on Democratic and Social Challenges*, edited by Esra Özyürek, Gaye Özpınar, and Emrah Altındiş. Switzerland: Springer.

Parmar, Pratibha. 1990. "Black Feminism: The Politics of Articulation." In *Identity: Community, Culture, Difference*, edited by Jonathan Rutherford, 101–26. London: Lawrence and Wishart.

Pösteki, Nigar. 2005. *1990 Sonrası Türk Sineması*. İstanbul: Es Yayınları.

Rancière, Jacques. 2009. *The Emancipated Spectator. Artforum International*. London, New York: Verso.

Rich, Adrienne. 1977. "It Is the Lesbian in Us." *Sinister Wisdom* 3.

Rocha, Glauber. 2019. "The Aesthetics of Hunger." *Film Manifestos and Global Cinema Cultures: A Critical Anthology*. Berkeley: University of California Press. https://doi.org/10.1525/9780520957411-068.

Saunders, Patricia J. 2008. "Fugitive Dreams of Diaspora: Conversations with Saidiya Hartman." *Anthurium: A Caribbean Studies Journal* 6 (1).

Saydam, Barış. 2021. "Türk Sinemasının Bağımsızlıkla İmtihanı." *Türk Sinema Araştırmaları*, 1–12.

Selek, Pınar. 2021. "What Do We Learn from the Feminist Movement in Turkey?" Turkey Beyond Borders. 2021.

Sharpe, Christina. 2016. *In the Wake: On Blackness and Being*. Durham, NC: Duke University Press.

Sharpe, Christina. 2023. *Ordinary Notes*. Toronto: Knopf Canada.

Shohat, Ella. 2001. *Taboo Memories, Diasporic Voices*. Durham, NC: Duke University Press.

Shohat, Ella. 2003. "Post-Third-Worldist Culture: Gender, Nation, and the Cinema." In *Rethinking Third Cinema*, edited by Anthony R. Guneratne and Wimal Dissanayake. New York and London: Routledge. https://doi.org/10.1017/CBO9781107415324.004.

Şimşek, Bahar, Özgür Çiçek, and Suncem Koçer. 2023. "Kürt Sineması Üzerine Bir Diyalog: Hakikat, Dil ve Yorum." *5 Harfliler*, December 2023.

Smelik, Anneke. 1998. *And the Mirror Cracked*. London: Macmillan Press.

Sönmez, Sevcan, and Hale Satıcı. 2019. *Kadının Kamerasından: 2000 Sonrası Kadın Yönetmenler*, edited by Sevcan Sönmez and Hale Satıcı. İstanbul: Doruk Yayınları.

Süalp, Zeynep Tül Akbal. 2009. "Unutmak İstemenin Boşluğunu Dolduranlar: Arabesk-Noir Ya Da Hiçlik Kutsamaları." In *V. Kültür Araştırmaları Sempozyumu*, 1–13. Zonguldak: Zonguldak Karaelmas Üniversitesi.

Süalp, Zeynep Tül Akbal. 2010. "Türkiye Sinemasının Dönemselleştirilmesi." *YeniFİLM*, no. 20: 35–41.

Suner, Asuman. 2006a. *Hayalet Ev Yeni Türk Sinemasında Aidiyet, Kimlik ve Bellek*. İstanbul: Metis Yayınları.

Suner, Asuman 2006b. "Outside in: 'Accented Cinema' at Large." *Inter-Asia Cultural Studies* 7 (3): 363–82. https://doi.org/10.1080/14649370600849223.

Suner, Asuman. 2007. "Cinema without Frontiers: Transnational Women's Filmmaking in Iran and Turkey." In *Transnational Feminism in Film and Media*, edited by Katarzyna Marciniak, Anikó Imre, and Áine O'Healy, 53–70. New York: Palgrave Macmillan. https://doi.org/10.1017/CBO9781107415324.004.

Suner, Asuman. 2010. *New Turkish Cinema: Belonging, Identity, And Memory*. New York: I. B. Tauris.

Surela Film. 2015. "Bakur." 2015. http://surelafilm.com/en/film-detay.aspx?id=17.

Susma Bitsin. 2022. "We Stand in Solidarity with Çiğdem Mater," April 2022.

T. C. Kültür ve Turizm Bakanlığı. 2004. "Sinema Filmlerinin Desteklenmesi Hakkında Yönetmelik." 2004. https://teftis.ktb.gov.tr/TR-14498/sinema-filmlerinin-desteklenmesi-hakkinda-yonetmelik.html.

T24. 2015. "Gösterimi Engellenen Bakur'un Yapımcısı Sansürün Adresini Gösterdi: Kültür Bakanlığı!" *T24*, April 12, 2015. https://t24.com.tr/haber/gosterimi-engellenen-pkk-belgesinin-yapimcisi-sansurun-adresini-gosterdi-kultur-bakanligi,293323.

Tanpınar, Ahmet Hamdi. 2013. *Günlüklerin Işığında Tanpınar'la Başbaşa*, edited by Zeynep Kerman and İnci Enginün. İstanbul: Dergah Yayınları.

Tanrıöver, Hülya Uğur. 2016. "Women as Film Directors in Turkish Cinema." *European Journal of Women's Studies* 24 (4): 321–35. https://doi.org/10.1177/1350506816649985.

Tolstoy, Leo. 1985. *Anna Karenina*. London: Penguin.

Trouillot, Michel-Rolph. 1995. *Silencing the Past: Power and the Production of History*. Boston: Beacon Press.

"Tunceli'de, 'Dersim'in Kayıp Kızları' Belgeselinin Galası Yapıldı." 2014. https://www.dailymotion.com/video/x2915gl.

Ustaoğlu, Yeşim. 2003. *Bulutları Beklerken (Waiting for the Clouds)*.

Vuong, Ocean. 2020. "Ocean Vuong: On Earth We're Briefly Gorgeous." Internationales Literaturfestival Berlin. 2020.

Vuong, Ocean. 2022. "Ocean Vuong: 'When I Write, I Feel Larger than the Limits of My Body.'" Louisiana Channel. 2022.

Weil, Simone. 2021. "Concerning the 'Our Father.'" In *Waiting for God*. New York: Routledge.

White, Patricia. 2015. *Women's Cinema, World Cinema Projecting Contemporary Feminisms*. Durham, NC, and London: Duke University Press.

Wilson, Elizabeth. 1991. *The Sphinx in the City: Urban Life, The Control of Disorder, and Women*. London: Virago Press. https://doi.org/10.2307/990818.

Wolff, Janet. 2004. "The Invisible Flaneuse: Women and the Literature of Modernity." In *Urban Culture Critical Concept in Literary and Cultural Studies*, edited by Chris Jenks. London, New York: Routledge.

Woolf, Virginia. 1942. *The Death of the Moth and Other Essays*. New York: Harcourt Inc.

Yalazan, Esra. 2013. "Hayat Ağacı – Hay Way Zaman." 2013. https://www.youtube.com/watch?v=1oDTbJihY7s.

Yamada, Mitsuye. 1981. "Invisibility Is an Unnatural Disaster: Reflections of an Asian American Woman." In *This Bridge Called My Back: Writings by Radical Women of Color*, edited by Cherríe Moraga and Gloria Anzaldúa, 35–41. New York: Kitchen Table: Women of Color Press.

Yaşartürk, Gül. 2014. "Çekirdek Ailenin Kabusları: 2000'li Yıllar Türkiye Sineması'nda Çekirdek Aileye Değişen Bakış." *Maltepe Üniversitesi İletişim Fakültesi Elektronik Dergisi*, 1–28.

Yaşartürk, Gül. 2017. "'Tereddüt': Eril Tahakkümün O Belirsiz Gölgesi." *Ayrıntıdergi*, January 2017. https://ayrintidergi.com.tr/tereddut-eril-tahakkumun-o-belirsiz-golgesi/.

Yetişkin, Ebru. 2010. "Güncel Politik Sinemayı Yeniden Düşünmek." *Akademik İncelemeler Dergisi* 5 (2): 95–116.

Yılmazok, Levent. 2010. "Turkish Films Co-Produced within Europe: The Story after Twenty Years' Experience in Eurimages." *SineCine* 1 (2): 87–108.

Zaim, Derviş. 2008. "Odaklandığın Şey Gerçeğindir: Türkiye Sineması, Alüvyonik Türk Sineması ve Uluslararası Kabul-2. Bölüm." *Altyazı* 79: 40–47.

Zihnioglu, Yaprak. 2003. *Kadinsiz İnkilap: Nezihe Muhiddin, Kadınlar Halk Fırkası, Kadın Birliği*. Istanbul: Metis Yayınları.

Index

EU Authorised Representative:
Easy Access System Europe Mustamäe tee 50, 10621 Tallinn, Estonia
gpsr.requests@easproject.com

Printed and bound by CPI Group (UK) Ltd, Croydon, CR0 4YY
29/09/2026
02224985-0001